LOST in the LONG WHITE CLOUD

Finding My Way Home

Conception
through the Death of My Father
Birth to Twenty-Nine Years

a memoir

David H. Rosen, MD

Rosenberry books, etc.

WIPF & STOCK · Eugene, Oregon

Also by David H. Rosen

Clouds and More Clouds

The Tao of Elvis

(a Rosenberry Books edition)

The Healing Spirit of Haiku

(with Joel Weishaus)

Evolution of the Psyche

(with Michael Luebbert)

The Tao of Jung: The Way of Integrity

Transforming Depression:

Healing the Soul Through Creativity

Medicine as a Human Experience

(with David Reiser)

Henry's Tower

(a children's book)

Lesbianism: A Study of Female Homosexuality

Part of chapter 1, "Conception, Birth and Mimi" was previously published in "Conception: The Tao is Operating," *Frogpond* 31.3 (2008):49.
Chapter 6: "Scent of spring … ," was originally published in *Modern Haiku* 38, No. 1 (2007): 67.

ISBN: 978-1-4982-0226-8

Designed by Rosenberry books, etc.
101 Nicks Bend West
Pittsboro, NC 27312
800.723.0336 919.969.2767
www.rosenberrybooks.com
Rosenberry books, etc. is a registered trademark.

Wipf & Stock is an imprint of Wipf and Stock Publishers.
199 W. 8th Ave., Suite 3
Eugene, OR 97401
wipfandstock.com

While all of the incidents in this book are true, some of the names and personal characteristics of the individuals involved have been changed.

Acknowledgements

I thank everyone who is a part of this work: especially my three lovely daughters Sarah, Laura and Rachel; my siblings Janet, Bill, Marti, and Nancy; my former wives Lynn and Debbie. I deeply appreciate my parents Barbara and Max, whose love made it all possible.

I am indebted to the Antioch Writer's Workshop in Yellow Springs, Ohio. Special thanks go to the angels who typed this manuscript: Adrianne Woodward in New Zealand; Patti Henderson in Texas; Joni DeForrest and Elizabeth Grosz in Oregon. A big thanks to Elizabeth, Ryan Novack and Susanne Petermann, who read what I wrote and provided valuable feedback. Another thanks to Alec Formatin Shirley for her assistance with the illustrations.

Heartfelt thanks to Lanara Sophia Emmanuel, my wife and soulmate. Her love and support has allowed me to complete this volume.

Finally, I feel deep gratitude to Diane and Philip at Rosenberry Books. I could not have imagined better midwives for this memoir.

Contents

Illustrations

Preface

The longest way round
is the shortest way home.

JAMES JOYCE
Ulysses

DAVID IN COPENHAGEN

Going to the Land of the Long White Cloud or *Aotearoa* (ah-o-teh-a-row-ah), the Maori name for New Zealand, had been a dream of mine for many years. In fact, I once considered applying for a job in Dunedin and immigrating to New Zealand. Although it took sixty years to be realized, the dream finally came true.

On Sunday, July 17, 2005 at 5:10 AM, I arrived in Auckland, New Zealand, the largest city on the North Island. It was a cold, dark, windy, rainy, dreary winter day. I'd left Texas two days earlier on a hot, bright summer afternoon, but everything in the Antipodes is reversed. In a short time I would fly to Christchurch, the main city on the colder South Island, where I would stay for five months while on sabbatical at the University of Canterbury. My objective was to do research on the healing value of personal narrative.[1] I planned to use the approach of a single case study in which the subject would be myself. So in a real way, my maxim "re-search is me-search" would be fulfilled.

On the long plane ride from Los Angeles, I sat next to Murray Jamieson, a firefighter. He represented New Zealand after 9/11. Murray went to Ground Zero in New York City and met President George Bush. He also organized the 2002 World Firefighters Games in Christchurch. Warm and friendly, he took it upon himself to shepherd me through customs in the international terminal at Auckland.

Despite the time and weather, his daughter and two of his grandchildren met us in the arrival area. Murray's daughter took us to her car, where her husband waited with their new baby. After loading up the luggage, they took us that morning to the domestic terminal for our seven o'clock flight to Christchurch. There I had my first "flat white" coffee. This gourmet beverage originated in Australia and New Zealand. It has a couple shots of espresso and well-frothed milk, usually with the design of a fern on the surface.

When we arrived in Christchurch at eight-thirty in the morning, I was very tired and jet-lagged. The person who was to meet me was not there, so Murray waited with me patiently, for forty minutes, until the absent-minded professor arrived. This faculty member was going to be gone for the same five-month period, in part for a sabbatical in England, so I had decided to rent his house. He let me use his car, as he lived thirty minutes outside of Christchurch.

After I said goodbye to Murray, the professor took me around the city and university but, given my condition, it unfortunately remains a blur. After the tour, he drove up Dyers Pass Road over the summit to Governors Bay. His six-year-old house was halfway up a hill. Sparsely furnished without a TV, computer or microwave, it was simple and rather monastic. The views from all the rooms and the little deck were spectacular. After I dropped him off at the airport, I had to find my way back. Driving on the left side of the road felt wrong. I was dazed and felt lost. Gradually, after several mistaken turns, I got back to my new abode.

So why come all the way to New Zealand, down under and upside-down? Because I wanted to be really lost so I could find my way home. The word *lost* derives from Old Norse and means *disbanding an army*, allowing one to strike "a truce with the wide world."[2] I came to this hillside house in order to find and make peace with my true self. I came to connect to an invisible spiritual force inside and outside myself. Taoism and Jung's psychology, both very influential in my life and work, focus on integrating opposites as a healing process toward wholeness.[3] Maybe I've come to New Zealand's more remote South Island, close to Antarctica, to reconcile something deep within myself.

This memoir is a good faith review of my life. It also contains dreams and experiences that I have recorded in journals from the age of eighteen. I offer up these stories — that sometimes seemed to write me, instead of the other way around — in the hope that they will be helpful to and embolden others. It is about my personal myth[4] and how my short life fits into the evolving tapestry of human stories.

While writing *The Healing Spirit of Haiku*, I was taken with the genre of *haibun*, prose combined with haiku, which is often about a journey.[5] In this volume, you will find the first part of my life-long pilgrimage. It has the same two goals, spiritual and practical, that Basho aimed to accomplish in his classic haibun *Narrow Road to the Interior*.[6] The spiritual goal is to glean the essence of my life's journey. The practical goal is to describe meaningful experiences; the more personal the experiences, the better, because then they are most archetypal or universal.

Why start my autobiography at age sixty? Gempo Yamamoto once said this to his student Soen Roshi: "At the age of sixty, one is more efficient than at fifty; seventy is more useful than sixty; eighty is more effective than seventy."[7] This quote inspires me, along with the life of my Kiwi poet friend Ralph Woodward who published a book of poetry at the age of eighty[8], to live at least another twenty years.[9]

I met Lanara, an American Kiwi, on a bench overlooking Governors Bay. I returned to the South Island during the summer of 2006 (*Aotearoa* winter) for two reasons: to see if we were compatible and to continue writing this book. We lived in a small house with a wood-burning stove in Purau. It was situated on a lovely quiet bay, just over the hill from Diamond Harbour. Lanara and I are now married and live in Oregon, the state in the United States most like New Zealand.

During my many years as a professor, it was natural to share a lot of myself in my teaching, analytic work and writing. Now, as a "recovering academic," I begin to tell the whole story.

Where to start?

Where else but at the beginning.

David H. Rosen
Governors Bay & Purau, New Zealand
College Station, Texas and Eugene, Oregon

NOTES

1 See James W. Pennebaker, *Opening Up: The Healing Power of Confiding in Others* (New York: Morrow, 1990); James W. Pennebaker, *Emotion, Disclosure, and Health* (Washington, DC: American Psychological Association, 1995); and Charles M. Anderson and Marian MacCurdy, eds., *Writing & Healing: Toward an Informed Practice* (Urbana, IL: National Council of Teachers of English, 2000).

2 Rebecca Solnit, *A Field Guide to Getting Lost* (New York: Viking, 2005).

3 David H. Rosen, *The Tao of Jung: The Way of Integrity* (New York: Penguin, 1997).

4 Personal myth, as described by Carl Jung in *Memories, Dreams, Reflections* (New York: Pantheon, 1963), involves the ego, the center of consciousness, and one's true authentic Self. In personal myth, the ego is secondary to the Self, which Jung called the *Imago Dei*: the center or image of God and the totality of the psyche.

5 David H. Rosen and Joel Weishaus, *The Healing Spirit of Haiku* (Berkeley, CA: North Atlantic Books, 2004). A second edition is being published by Rosenberry Books.

6 Matsuo Basho, *Basho's Narrow Road: Narrow Road to the Interior*, trans. Hiroaki Sato (Berkeley, CA: Stone Bridge Press, 1996), 18.

7 Soen Nakagawa, *Endless Vow: The Zen Path of Soen Nakagawa*, trans. and eds. Kazuaki Tanahashi and Sherry Chayat (Boston: Shambhala Publications, 1996), 8.

8 Ralph Woodward, *Silverfish & Slate Pencils* (Christchurch, New Zealand: Cygnet, 2005).

9 My physical therapist, Erik Verdouw, says that I'll live to ninety-six, but I would be thrilled with eighty-eight.

For my grandsons: Aidan and Benjamin

The truth is the kindest thing we can give folks
in the end.

HARRIET BEECHER STOWE
The Pearl of Orr's Island:
A Story of the Coast of Maine

LOST in the LONG WHITE CLOUD

Finding My Way Home

a memoir

Conception through the Death of My Father

Birth to Twenty-Nine Years

People like you and me, though mortal, of course, like everyone else, do not grow old no matter how long we live. What I mean is that we never cease to stand like curious children before the great Mystery into which we are born.

ALBERT EINSTEIN
from a letter to Otto Juliusburger,
September 29, 1942

1

Conception, Birth and Mimi

The beginning
is the most important part of the work.

PLATO
The Republic, Book I. 377b

Flowering tree
showered with mist —
smile on my face

PARENTS IN LOVE

I asked my mentally clear ninety-two year old mother, that year before she died, to tell me about where I was conceived and what it was like. I didn't expect her to go back to the moment when one of my father's sperms was penetrating one of my mother's eggs. Bottom line: I wondered if I was conceived in love.

To my surprise I learned that, although my parents fought a lot in married life and were divorced from each other twice, I was the product of love-making. This gave me a warm feeling inside. How wonderful!

But the shocker was where I was conceived: the old Taos Inn in Taos, New Mexico. This is a place where I have stayed and made love to many women. All of this love-making, then, has a very meaningful history. My father Max, a navy physician, was on leave from the marines before being shipped out to the Pacific during WWII. My mother traveled by car to Albuquerque from Kansas City with her mother, Ethel Bown, and my two-month-old sister, Janet. My mother, Barbara Jane, then drove alone to Taos for a romantic interlude with my father. So I was conceived in love, when my father was truly himself, before he was injured in the war.

Not knowing why, I kept returning to Taos. When I was a boy, I went there with my family as part of a vacation. I recall visiting the same *pueblo* that Carl Jung went to when he had his meaningful conversations with Chief Mountain Lake.[1] I went to Taos as a young, middle-aged, and old man. I even attempted to buy property there after spending some time in Taos with a Jungian analyst and his lovely family. He had built a beautiful home there, and I wondered if Taos would support another Jungian analyst. Now I know why I repeatedly went to Taos, which interestingly, has the word *Tao* in its name.

At 12:32 PM on February 25, 1945, David Henry, a war baby, was born to a lonely, stressed, overworked social worker; a mother already saddled with an eleven-month-old daughter. Fortunately, my mother hired Mimi to take care of me from the time I was born until age two. Mimi left me to care for the baby of one of her five daughters. I didn't, however, learn about Mimi until I was thirty-six years old.

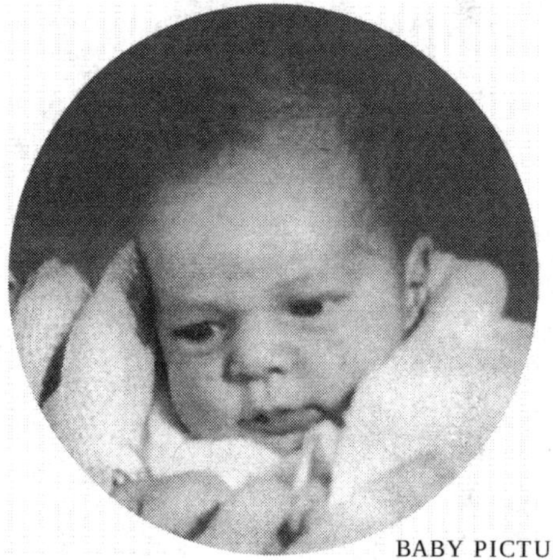

BABY PICTURE

When I was born, the Red Cross attempted to find my father to give him the good news. The message my mother got back was: "Missing in action." My father was island-hopping in the Pacific with the marines, on their way to Iwo Jima. He was evacuated as shell shocked and later received a purple heart. He never fully recovered. His war wound was inadvertently transferred to me and was at the core of my becoming a conscientious objector at age eighteen.

When my mother took me home from the hospital in Port Chester, New York, Mimi cared for me. In 1938 my parents purchased Bright Bank, a large manor house on the Boston Post Road in the village of Rye, where I have cherished memories. It was the former residence of Civil War Union General, Caleb Henry Carlton.

In the darkness,
Bright Bank glowed—
Mimi's smile

During the early summer of 1981 I was visiting my mother in Springfield, Missouri. We were in the library, and I was sitting next to my older sister looking through a family photo album of our early years in Rye, New York. There were many pictures of Janet and me playing together, picking flowers or just holding hands. I thanked her for being there for me and conveyed that if it hadn't had been for her, I'd probably be on a back ward in some mental hospital. She said, "It wasn't me, it was Mimi."

Janet showed me Mimi's photo. She looked vaguely familiar like a great-aunt; I always thought she was one of our relatives. Janet said Mimi took care of me from birth until age two. I asked my mother if this was true. She said Yes. I asked, "Why didn't you ever tell me about her?" She answered, "I thought you knew."

I had not known … suddenly my stomach felt queasy. I inquired if Mimi was still alive and asked where she lived. My mother said she heard from her every Christmas, and she always asked about me. Mimi was eighty-seven and lived in an assisted living residence in Hudson, Minnesota, not far from Saint Paul. I got her phone number, called, and arranged to visit her.

The love Mimi had given me pulled me to

her. She was like a kind-hearted grandmother whom I had not seen in over thirty years. Within a few days I was at her door. On my way, I surmised that my mother never told me about Mimi because she felt guilty that she had not taken care of me as an infant. However, I felt wonderful that she had gotten Mimi to attend to me and that I'd found out in time to visit her.

After I saw Mimi and entered her apartment, I understood the role she had played in my attraction to the spiritual. On the wall was a sign, "God is Love." Mimi was short and thin, with a full head of white hair. The first thing she said after we embraced was, "I've been praying for you to return." She thought my mother had informed me that she wanted to hear from me and, if possible, see me. Now it didn't matter. Her prayers were answered.

We talked for many hours. She explained that she stopped caring for me when her oldest daughter had her first child. She didn't want to leave me, but felt that she had to. Mimi had five daughters and had been deserted by her husband when they were all under ten years old. She was so distraught and depressed when it happened that she became suicidal. However, this was for her a spiritual and transformative experience. It was uncanny that I had had a similar experience, which led to my research on depression and suicide.[2]

Happiness —
bright red hibiscus
opens

I immediately recognized Mimi as a second mother, and I will never forget the sparkle and hope in her eyes and the warmth of her smile. She said, "You are so precious to me. You are the son I always wanted, and now you have come home." That night we went out to the best restaurant in Hudson and continued to catch up on our lives. I shared photos and stories about Debbie, my wife at the time, and our daughter Sarah. Then she went to the restroom and paid the bill before I could. Later I asked to repay her. She said, "No, it's my treat." When I asked why, she replied, "Because I love you."

Being reunited with Mimi was one of the peak experiences of my life. When writing about this, and rereading it, I cried. I recalled Tu Fu's words: "People with feeling must shed tears. Water flows on, and blossoms fade."[3] I've often reflected with great tenderness on the first two years of my life, which, according to Erik Erikson, is when the seeds of trust, hope and faith are sown. When nurtured, they develop into love, integrity, and wisdom.[4]

Walking alone
with my friend
white butterfly

NOTES

1 Carl Jung, *Memories, Dreams, Reflections* (New York: Pantheon, 1963).

2 David H. Rosen, *Transforming Depression: Healing the Soul through Creativity* (York Beach, ME: Nicolas-Hays, 2002).

3 In this book Du Fu is spelled *Tu Fu*. Tu Fu was a Chinese Poet (712-770) who influenced Basho (1644-1694), and other Japanese poets. See *Poetry and Prose of the Tang and Song*, trans. Xianyi Yang and Gladys Yang (Beijing, China: Panda Books, 2005), 46.

4 Erik Erikson, *Life Cycle Completed* (New York: W.W. Norton, 1982).

2

Discord: Loss and Confusion

In probing my childhood (which is the next best thing to probing one's eternity), I see the awakening of consciousness as a series of spaced flashes, with the intervals between them gradually diminishing until bright blocks of perception are formed, affording memory a slippery hold.

VLADIMIR NABOKOV
Speak memory: An Autobiography Revisited

Mimi left six months after my troubled father came home from the mental hospital. It was a poorly timed coming and going. Even now it is difficult for me to face feelings of loss and abandonment, and being divorced by my second wife in 1994 caused me unprecedented despair. Yet I am beginning to resolve and accept the horrendous pain that it caused me and my three daughters by forcing myself to be lost in New Zealand and writing this memoir. Ending up with women who leave me has been an agonizing pattern, and I finally realized that I either picked women who would leave me or whom I would leave. Nevertheless, I'm sure that my ability to love women stems from the unconditional love I received from both Mimi and my mother. The key to giving love has been loving my self … my soul.

When Mimi left, my mother, then a beautiful, tall and fiercely independent career woman, stayed at home and cared for her two toddlers and a mentally-ill husband, unable to work at the time. My mother had also suffered an early loss. Her beloved father Karl Middendorf (endearingly called Pops), of German background, divorced her mother, Ethel Bown of English and Scots-Irish stock, when my mother was just thirteen years old and her only sister, Martha, was seven. In a way, that hardship made her stronger. After graduating from college, which was uncommon for women in the mid-1930s though her mother likewise graduated from college, she ventured off to New York City alone to pursue a graduate education, which was also rare for women at that time. She obtained a Master's in Social Work from Columbia University.

My father, Max, was handsome, tall, bright, and accomplished. He grew up on the lower east side of Manhattan in a poor Jewish immigrant neighborhood. He was the only son among four children. He had an older sister, Frimi, and two younger identical twin sisters, Ruth and Esta. His optimistic and hard-working Romanian father, Abraham, was born in Bucharest and was an actor in the Yiddish Theater, turned tailor. Abraham's father Sander was a pastry chef for King Carol I of Romania, and his blind wife Rose was his taster. My father's Romanian mother, Kadie, was from Iasi and was melancholic. She never forgave her only son for marrying a gentile. She refused to greet my mother when we visited, and we had to go into the kitchen to see her. Even though I was very young, I had the sense of how odd this was! My Dad went to the City College of New York on a full scholarship. He was one of the few Jewish students in the 1930s at Cornell University Medical College in New York City. He excelled in medical school and, prior to WW II, was a fully trained physician and surgeon and a board certified eye, ear, nose, and throat specialist. When the war started, he enlisted in the navy and was a member of a court-martial board, until he was deployed for combat in 1944. He completed basic training with the Marines at Camp Pendleton in California.

Both my parents, despite being very intelligent, were emotionally distant and detached, my mother by temperament and my father due to a war injury. Neither parent hugged us or said I love you. However, they were both kind and generous in their own ways. They encouraged our spiritual development. My mom was friendly to nearly everyone. My dad took us fishing and camping, as well as hunting for arrowheads and rocks. Nevertheless, my earliest years took place in a cold and stressful environment, especially after the warmth of Mimi disappeared. From that point on, I believe that Janet's presence saved me from ending up like either parent. Yet I have done my best to incorporate positive aspects of both my mother and father, such as their love for education, humanity, healing, culture, science, history, and artistic pursuits.

One of my clearest and darkest memories, from around the age of three-and-a-half, was late at night holding hands with Janet and wandering through our huge house without finding either parent at home. I remember feeling scared and walking hand-in-hand down the steep pitch-black gravel driveway to the house of our neighbor, Della La Blanche. After knocking on the door, she opened it and took us in. What a relief! This took place several other times as well, and I've often wondered what would have happened to us without Della. Finding no parent at home reoccurred when I was ten in Springfield, Missouri. However, that time I called the police, who came and stayed to raise my parents' consciousness about leaving five children under the age of eleven home alone without a baby-sitter.

WITH JANET IN RYE

Because of the war, my father acquired an explosive temper with violent outbursts. When I finally met Mimi again, one of the things I asked her about was my father and whether he ever hurt me. She said he never hit me, but he would yell and knock things over that I built. Mimi's perspective of this chaotic and disorganized situation brought back other distressing memories. They eventually became the basis for my children's book, *Henry's Tower*.[1]

These recollections raise issues of lack of oversight and carelessness. Although, as the father of three children, I know how easy it is to lose track of one's kids, especially when there is more than one under the age of three or four. My mother transposed such memories into the humorous stories she told at family gatherings, but as we know from the Greeks, on the other side of comedy is tragedy.

There is another story of when I was also three-and-a-half years old that tells of early consciousness. I got up very early one morning, before my sister and parents, put a chair up to the kitchen counter, got down a box of corn flakes, and made a trail to my parents' bedroom door. Following this, I took out milk and sugar, then poured and sprinkled these over the track of breakfast cereal. This radical and symbolic art-of-protest did make an impression on my parents, my mother in particular.

Peonies under
shade of yellow roses —
no one home

My mother arranged for tree work on the tall pines in our front yard. The workers left a fully extended thirty-foot ladder up against one of the trees where they had been trimming limbs. Being a curious and adventuresome four-year-old, I climbed up to the top of the ladder — what fun! How exhilarating to climb so high! Luckily at the moment my mother found me, she was wise enough not to yell. She leaned stiffly on the ladder. Looking right at me, she gently called my name, “David, please come down the same way you got up there. Hold on and step down one step at a time. Good boy!” I recall thinking that it was odd, or counterintuitive, that she didn’t climb up to get me. Now I understand that her neurotic fear of heights froze her at the bottom. She patiently, yet miraculously, talked me down. My mother was an almost non-stop talker, but she held your attention! I remember the big and rare embrace I got when she took me off the ladder.

This incident illustrates a lot about me, and I’ve been climbing ladders unafraid ever since. These ladders include college, medical school, internship, residency in psychiatry, chief residency, medical licenses and specialty board exams, academic tenure track, and training to become a Jungian psychoanalyst. There have also been the ladders of painting, haiku poetry, relationships with women, parenting children, and mentoring students and grandchildren. Throughout my life I’ve paid therapists (individual and marital) and psychoanalysts (Freudian, Jungian and Kleinian) to help talk me down! At this point in my life, I know Lao Tzu was right when he said, “Whether you go up the ladder or down it, your position is shaky. When you stand with your two feet on the ground, you will always keep your balance.”[2]

Another remembrance concerns an artistic seed that has flourished, grown and developed over the years. I thank my very talented and gifted parents for encouraging and modeling for me that art is healing. My mother wrote poetry and made quilts, wall hangings and stained glass windows. Before my father's untimely death at the age of sixty-five, he painted, carved stone and made jewelry. The first time I recall creating art was around age four when I melted crayons on the radiators in my room. It was pure frolic, an entertaining diversion! The designs and colors surely gave rise to my later bright abstract paintings, as in "Triptych" (see flyleaves), created while I was in medical school.

A different memory, at times offset by melted crayons, was the smell of urine-soaked sheets on my bed and hanging around my room to dry. Maybe this was why our dog, Buzz Fuzz, used to love to stay in my room. For all I know some of the piss might have been his! In all seriousness, Buzz Fuzz provided unconditional love and was the basis of friendship that I found with other dogs throughout my life. Upon reflection, I thought of Soen Nakagawa Roshi's haiku: [3]

Buddha nature
of a dog, a human
in full bloom

There are actually more positive memories than negative. There were lots of toys, and I often played with Janet. When it was warm, we played outside in the sandbox or with our wagons and push carts. At other times, we observed, smelled or picked the many flowers that my mother planted and loved. I can still see and smell those lilacs, roses and peonies. Because of this experience, Janet and I now both raise and arrange flowers. In addition, our backyard contained a gigantic rock that we often played on. I remember climbing it as if it were a mountain. I started doing this when I was three and kept at it until we moved to Texas. When just four years old, I recall the thrill and sense of accomplishment I felt when I first reached the top. It was very important for me to reach the summit. My desire to climb anything and reach the top was an early indication of my ambitious nature.

Lilacs blossom
birds fly north —
dream of a mountain to climb

NOTES

1 David H. Rosen, *Henry's Tower* (Pittsford, NY: Platypus Books, 1984). A second edition will also be published by Rosenberry Books.

2 Lao Tzu, *Tao Te Ching*, trans. Steven Mitchell (New York: HarperCollins, 1988), Chapter 13.

3 Soen Nakagawa, *Endless Vow: The Zen Path of Soen Nakagawa*, trans. and ed. by Kazuaki Tanahashi and Sherry Chayat (Boston: Shambhala Publications, 1966), 130.

3

Big Spring, Texas

All life is an experiment.

RALPH WALDO EMERSON
Journals of Ralph Waldo Emerson: With Annotations, Volume 6

In 1949, Big Spring, Texas, had one paved road: the highway. Big Spring is between Sweetwater, to the east, and Midland, to the west. In order to get a job in his specialty, my father had to take a position anywhere he could. An opening happened to be at the Veteran's Hospital in Big Spring, which was in the middle of nowhere. Consequently, we headed to desolate, yet wild, West Texas. On reflection, what he did was ingenious. The old wounded navy physician "died" in New York and the new, healing physician and surgeon was reborn in a desert. He started his new job on July 1, 1949 in a place which is, as far as the temperature is concerned, the beginning of hell on earth. It is usually over a hundred degrees (Fahrenheit) throughout the summer and into most of September, when it starts to cool down. There were also blustery winds, sand storms and harsh winters, which included heavy rain, sleet and snow. In New York, when I turned five, I would have gone to kindergarten. The problem was that Big Spring didn't have a kindergarten! You need plentiful water for any kind of garden; in Big Spring there were only tumbleweeds and sand. Historically there was a big spring, but when we were there, no such spring existed.

My mother was also going through a death and rebirth experience. She was pregnant and had bought into the American Dream of the working father and the stay-at-home mother. Janet had started the first grade, so my mother was stuck with only me at home, and I was a handful. The desert was my playground, and I became the leader of a little neighborhood gang composed of two five-year-olds: a girl named Anne and a boy called José. Our play was to head into the desert to catch horned toads, which looked like little iguanas, and bring them home for pets. We also had wrestling matches out in the wild, learning what happens when you run into, or fall on, cacti! I recall the painful hours it took for my mother to extract the sharp needles that hooked themselves into the skin on my arms, legs, feet, and buttocks! There was no Buzz Fuzz. He was killed on Boston Post Road before we left — what a sacrifice! I was so stunned that I wouldn't eat the day that he died. I'll never forget his burial near the enormous rock nor the stream of tears that ran down my face. Nevertheless, we did have a dog that wandered into our lives in Texas.

I also remember the beer parties held in our backyards. Anne, José and I must have known about the association between beer and parties. We shook the cans we got out of our parents' refrigerators and opened them with sharp rocks — wow, the explosions and geysers of white foam! The goal was to see who could get the snowy spray to go the highest and all over each other. The glee we felt was not shared by our parents, especially our mothers, who always found out first.

Hanging on the front porch railing at José's house were shiny red peppers. They looked sweet, and I was tricked by José into eating some. Little did I know that they were hot chili peppers! I recall running home with my mouth on fire. I spent hours sucking ice cubes, and I couldn't talk or sleep that night. I was so miserable that I didn't eat any kind of red peppers for at least twenty years.

EASTER BEST

How did my mother handle it all, especially as she approached her last trimester? How did she break up the tiny gang of three? As autumn neared, she decided in her wisdom, or desperation, to enroll me in a tap dancing class.

It sounds fine, but my teacher, from New Jersey, was a divorced, middle-aged alcoholic. The dance room was messy and smelled like a

AT HOME IN BIG SPRING

trash heap. There were six kids around five years of age, in the two-and-a half hour class. Held Monday through Friday, it functioned as a kind of crude daycare. During the class the teacher played music, supposedly to accompany our tap dancing. If she was able, she would show us steps and moves on the dirty linoleum floor. Sometimes, however, she just sat there dazed or asleep on the frayed couch. Reflecting back on this, she probably had black-out spells. Little did our parents know, or want to know....

As kids, we loved the frenzied play and dance time. Did I learn tap dancing? Well, if I get really drunk, I can do what seems like the rudiments of tap dancing. But in those moments, who cares? I have jokingly said that I'm a Jungian psychoanalyst because of this experience, but it actually goes back to what was suffered long before I got to Big Spring.

Ah, Big Spring, where a wild horse stuck its head in a screenless open window in the living room. It stayed there a while and sort of smiled. I also remember the creative fun of decorating a six-foot-tall tumbleweed as our Christmas Tree in 1949.

One week later on December 31, 1949, my brother, William Karl, was born. Bill is the only real Texan in our family. Left alone with my sister Janet, I remember watching a primitive TV and waiting up to see our new baby brother in a big news story. Anticipating that Bill would be the first baby born in the new decade of the

1950s, my father went to be with my mother and new brother at the hospital. Actually, he was the last baby born in 1949. My mother couldn't wait the necessary seven more minutes. They never appeared on TV, and we fell asleep as the New Year was celebrated.

Now we were a family of five. My father had fulfilled his minimal one-year commitment at the Veteran's Hospital, and on May 31, 1950, he gave one-month notice that he was resigning. We headed east to Kansas City, Missouri, where my mother's parents lived. Her father, "Pops," a successful civil engineer, and "Moms," his kind and lovely former secretary, lived in a new, large, fancy yet warm home in the country. They had beautiful flower and vegetable gardens, as well as fruit trees. My mother's matriarchal family — her mother Ethel, maternal grandmother Delilah, and sister Martha — lived together in the kind of small, pleasant suburbian home which became stereotypically American by the end of the 1950s.

My time in Texas reflected the "death" of another young ego identity and the coming transformation in Missouri. Santoka, the modern Japanese haiku poet, captured my Big Spring experience:[1]

This is the dance of butterflies
before death.

Searching for water in the desert —
Big Spring, Texas
fades in the distance

NOTES

1 James Abrams, "Hail in the Begging Bowl: The Odyssey and Poetry of Santoka," *Monumenta Nipponica* 32 (1997): 301.

4

Settling in Missouri

Sitting quietly, doing nothing.
Spring comes and the grass grows
by itself.

ZEN VERSE
from the *Zenrin Kushû*[1]

MOMS AND POPS

It was wonderful spending time with Moms and Pops. Moms was very loving, like Mimi, and Pops was kind and funny. They were affectionate and warmhearted. Their home was welcoming, stable and surrounded by nature. I recall picking flowers, which was one of my favorite things to do. I also remember gathering vegetables with Moms that she would later prepare for dinner. It was a delight to harvest peaches and help Moms bottle them. Both Moms and Pops had a way of including us in their chores and making it fun and exciting. They told us stories at night. When we couldn't go to sleep, it was okay to get up and go outside with them while they watered the garden, lawn and fruit trees. It was a magical time because I could just sit, be happy and watch the stars.

Nature:
flowers, fruits and vegetables …
home on earth

Meanwhile, in the suburban dwelling, I remember my great-grandma, with her white hair and gold wire-rimmed glasses, staring at me. She was usually sitting in her rocking chair in the living room, like an elderly Duchess overseeing her domain. At noon every day, she commanded me to bring her a glass of milk toast. Neither she nor my grandma seemed happy. At my maternal grandmother's home, I felt out-numbered. It felt like a controlled environment. My Aunt Martha was more cheerful, but she worked a lot as did my grandma. To my aunt's and grandmother's credit, they planned special activities for us, like going to the Kansas City Blues baseball games or, if there was a play suitable for children, to the Starlight Theater. We looked forward to these special events.

When school started, Janet and Terry, a six-year-old neighbor boy who lived across the back fence, were gone. During the days, I then often sat quietly and read National Geographic magazines while my great-grandmother took naps. For some unknown reason, Janet continued in school but I, to my disappointment, was kept out when I ought to have been in kindergarten. Looking back on it now, I wonder what the reason for this might have been.

In the evenings we played board games, like Parcheesi, or simple card games, like Old Maid. It was a hush-hush, neat-and-keep-quiet home, the opposite of the freedom and come-and-go nature of being in the country with Moms and Pops. Many times I'd ask if I could go and play with Terry, but only sometimes were my requests granted. I liked Terry's house, even though it was messy and noisy with three other kids, a dog and a cat. It was warm, and I liked being around his mother and father, who seemed to love each other and their children.

THE MATRIARCHY

Open door to dark room
watching the clock —
feeling uprooted

While Janet and I alternated between my two maternal grandparents' homes, my parents and my baby brother were searching for a place to settle down. Finally in Springfield, Missouri, gateway to the Ozarks, my father found an eye, ear, nose, and throat practice he wanted to take over. Both my mother and father liked this small community of around fifty thousand people in 1950. Springfield had several colleges and hospitals, as well as one high school appropriately named Central. It was the only city in Southwest Missouri, so it was predicted to grow and develop. However, it was in the South and only a hundred miles from Arkansas. During the Civil War, Missouri was a divided state and the southern part fought for the Confederacy. Hence in Springfield there was overt segregation, and Lincoln was the all-black school for the first through twelfth grades.

When we moved to Springfield, we rented a very small house behind a skating rink. Compared to Texas, it felt weird to be cramped together in such a tiny space. Fortunately, we were only there for a short time. We soon moved to a large house on the north side of town, on Washington Street near Boyd Elementary School. We lived there from 1950 to 1952, and I went to a real school for the first time. I was enrolled in the second grade, so I was in the same classroom as my sister Janet.

SPRINGFIELD, AGE SIX, SECOND GRADE

Mrs Hays was our teacher, and I was a problem student. There was competition and tension with my sister, and I didn't know all the things that the other students knew. I had never been to kindergarten or first grade, and I didn't know my abc's perfectly or how to count as well as the other children. Despite these hurdles, I learned quickly and caught up with the others. Janet shined, so at the end of that year my parents decided to have her skip the third grade and go right into the fourth grade with Mrs Wingo. In part their decision was based on the theory, probably correct, that some of my difficulties stemmed from sibling rivalry.

I remember a fairly stable home for those two years. My dad went to work and my mom stayed home, cooked and cleaned. But she soon got help when my second sister, Martha Anne (Marti), was born October 21, 1951. I recall the pleasing rituals that came with our first Christmas and Hanukkah. There was no distinct difference between the two holidays for me, and it meant spending wonderful times together as a family. My father educated us about Jewish holidays, and we went to the small synagogue of eighty families and to the affiliated Jewish Community Center. I also recollect playing Canasta with my sister, mother and father. My dad taught me to play chess, which I still enjoy. It was complicated, and he would not let me win. This allowed me to learn the game, as he was a master.

On my first day in third grade, my teacher, Miss Neff, called the roll and asked us to raise our hands if we were present. She mispronounced my name, calling out "David Raisin." Although I slowly put my hand up, I was too embarrassed to tell her about it. After class, however, I quietly went to her and said that my name was David Rosen. She apologized and didn't get it wrong again. I loved school and I worked hard at moving to the top quarter of the class. My parents, who valued education, helped with homework and special projects.

We moved to a nicer house at 1350 East Walnut Street. Our new school was McDaniel Elementary. Janet was in the fifth grade with Miss Miller, and I started the fourth grade with

Miss Greer. I continued to thrive both at school and at home. I was shy and making new friends was difficult. But I did make friends with, for example, a boy named Roger.

One of the things my parents accomplished that was very important to me, then and throughout my life, was to form a Unitarian Universalist Fellowship with four other families. Many of the children in the Fellowship provided a continuity of friends and a larger spiritual community that was, in many ways, an extended family. Later, when I would visit my oldest sister and brother who remained in Springfield, I would often reconnect with members of that original fellowship.

During the summer of 1953, we bought the old Wells family home at 900 East Walnut Street, on the corner of Dollison Street. It was a large three-story house with a big yard and barn. Much later it became a registered historic site and a bed and breakfast called the Walnut Street Inn, with all previous owners having rooms named after them. The Rosen Room was my old bedroom!

Finally, we could get all of our furniture from Bright Bank out of storage. The house was elegant, warm and cozy. In addition, every child had his or her own room. I have fond memories of that house, and many dreams, from the time I started recording them, take place there. On November 2, 1953 my third sister, Nancy Deborah, was born.

I was nine years old the night I dreamt that God, a very old man with white hair and a beard, looked into the microspcope my father had given me. He gazed into a drop of water on the slide and said, “Our universe is only one of many.” I’ve never forgotten this experience.

My mom had the following nicknames for us starting with Nancy and going up to Janet: Little Baby, Baby, Bitsy, Butch, and Wolfie. Over the seven years we lived in that house, I remember my mom hollering all five nicknames out the back door, calling us to come in and eat dinner! The Horners, who lived next door, had ten children. As a result, we always had ample playmates for hide and seek, red rover and many sports, especially basketball. My dad had a basketball hoop put up for us, and he used to play the game of horse with my brother and me. Actually, we all developed pretty good shots.

I started the fifth grade with Miss Miller at McDaniel Elementary School, while my sister had the renowned Mrs Murphy for sixth grade. She was known to give all A's to every child in her class, for which she was loved by students but disliked, even hated, by other teachers.

I, however, suffered a traumatic experience in Miss Miller's class that I've never gotten over. She said that I couldn't carry a tune, and, at our Thanksgiving-day choir concert, I was told to pull the stage curtain! I still have trouble singing. It wasn't until 1999, when I was on sabbatical in Japan, that I ws able to make some headway on this issue. Singing karaoke while drinking, I could belt out songs for the first time in my life. It was amazing! My Japanese friends and colleagues said I was a good singer, but they too had been consuming a fair amount of alcohol.… At any rate, although I never did it, I always said that I wanted to form a rock and roll band called "Miss Miller's Thanksgiving Day Choir Drop Out Band."[2] I imagined myself as the lead singer and used to say that I would find Miss Miller and give her the performance of a lifetime.

There was a bright spot in the fifth grade: my first serious girlfriend, Trudie Rose. I even had her name carved on my yo-yo, which was the craze at the time. She lived near me on Dollison Street, so we spent a lot of time together especially during early summer after the fifth grade ended. She was the first girl I ever kissed, and it was pleasurable, maybe in part because it was the original merest touch. I remember thinking that if we got married all she would have to do is add an *n* to her last name. She was pretty and fun to be with, but we broke up when she moved away before starting the sixth grade.

On path
from desert to plains —
alight in Springfield

NOTES

1 As Alan Watts describes in *The Way of Zen* (Part 1, chapter 4: "The Rise and Development of Zen,"151), the *Zenrin Kushu* is an anthology of five thousand two-line poems, compiled by Toyo Eicho (1429–1504) from Chinese sources: Buddhist, Taoist, classical literature, popular songs, etc. The *Zenrin Kushu* was used as a source-book for Zen students, who would select verses expressing the theme of a newly solved koan, as required by their masters.

2 Chris Hopwood called his band by this name. Chris thought that I could sing and helped me copyright my first song, "Where Elvis Lives." I wrote this song for Patti Henderson, my PhD student and graduate assistant for seven years, after she went to Memphis for her internship at a VA medical center. "Where Elvis Lives" is now available on iTunes. It is performed by Chris Hopwood and Miranda Zent.

5

Embraced by Mrs Murphy

The giving of love is an education in itself.

ELEANOR ROOSEVELT

Based on the Brown v. Board of Education Supreme Court decision during the summer of 1955, the public schools of Springfield prepared to quietly integrate. As school time neared, I recall my mother saying, "You and Joe will both go to McDaniel Elementary School this year."

Joe and I had been friends for two summers. During the previous year I had trouble understanding why he couldn't attend the fifth grade at McDaniel, since he lived only half a block from the school. He was sent across town to the segregated Lincoln School, which was now going to be remodeled and turned into the new Eastwood Junior High School that both Joe and I would attend the following year. Now Joe would go to his neighborhood school and have Mrs Murphy for a teacher! She would have a huge impact on his life, as well as on every other student in her class.

Racial discrimination is very difficult, if not impossible, for children to understand and accept. To me Joe was simply my friend, not a black boy or someone who was different from any of my other friends. Prejudice is not the purview of open-minded children but rather the predilection of close-minded adults. In reflecting on this vital matter, Sosan's words come to mind, "To perceive reality as it is, is to live with an open mind."[1]

On the first day of school, there was the usual mix of students: smart, motivated, unmotivated, dull, troublemakers, and troubled. There was a feeling of suspense that day in class, as we'd all heard about Mrs Murphy. She was middle-aged, of medium height and sturdy, with graying brown hair, a kind face, soulful eyes, and a big warm smile. She was quiet, and we got quiet. When it was silent, she spoke, "I'm sure you've all heard about me and that I give all A's. Well, it's true. However, you'll all work hard and deserve the A's I give you. It sounds strange, but it isn't. I love children, but I don't have any of my own. So you are my children, and I'll treat you that way. This is an important year before you leave McDaniel Elementary School and enter Eastwood Junior High School. So let's get started. You know me, and now I want to get to know you."

She began with the student on the first row to her left. It was Roger, an average student, who, although my friend, was also a trouble-maker. She asked him and each of the next twenty-four students to stand up, say their name and the things they liked in and out of school. Roger said that he didn't like school, but outside of school he liked baseball and riding his bike. Then she hugged Roger and said, "I love you. I'm going to help you like school as much as you like baseball and riding your bike." She commenced to do the same thing with every other student. It was genuine, and we knew we were hers and she loved us.

Mrs Murphy helped all students, including Joe who had only made D's and a few C's before at Lincoln, to love themselves, learn as much as they could and build confidence. The A's were given when you worked to your fullest aptitude. Mrs Murphy was way ahead of her time in that she tailored her class to each student's abilities and needs. Bottom line: love works! She had harmony in her classroom, and everyone worked hard for their A's.

In homage to Basho, who wrote a haiku about seeing the face of God in an opening flower:

In the opening roses,
the face of God —
remembering Mrs Murphy

In the sixth grade I did not have any girlfriends, maybe because I basked in Mrs Murphy's love. However, I had a date with the singer Brenda Lee, before she became famous. My sister was friends with Linda Sosbee. Her father, Tommy Sosbee, was part of Red Foley's Ozark Jubilee, a country music show on TV that originated in Springfield. Linda knew Brenda and arranged the big date. My mother drove us to the Fox Theater on the square for a movie on a Saturday afternoon. Brenda Lee was petite, as I was then, and shy like me. It was a blind date: tense, polite and not very much fun.

In Mrs Murphy's class, I started to feel good about myself and work to my capacity. Before then I lacked confidence, in part because my troubled father would sometimes snap and call me "stupid." He did this once, for example, when I couldn't figure out simple division problems. My mother overcompensated by telling me that I was very smart and could do anything I wanted. When this view of my mother's joined with Mrs Murphy's precept, I took off.

Just before the school year ended, I went alone to see Elvis Presley perform at The Shrine Mosque Auditorium. I sat near the front and was overwhelmed by the way he sang and moved. Pulsating with rhythm and blues, he seemed primitive but, at the same time, pure and spiritual. It was as if a genie was released from the conservative, segregated, conformist bottle of 1950s culture. Experiencing Elvis at that time made a deep and lasting impression on my life.[2]

I'll never forget the party that Mrs Murphy gave at her home on the afternoon and evening of the last day of school. She and her equally kind husband had a cook-out for us and our parents. Mrs Murphy made a special dessert of hot fudge sundaes for everyone. She took the time to introduce each of us to her husband, and she met everyone's parents. With her arm around each student, she told all of the parents what she told my parents: how much she loved each child, and how proud she was of each of them.

When we finally left, she gave every student a big hug and kiss on the cheek. She asked us to stay in touch and come back and see her. During the year many former students had done just that. Roger ended up as a college-educated businessman, and Joe graduated from Central High School, becoming a foreman at a local factory and an acclaimed singer. I, too, kept Mrs Murphy apprised of my accomplishments over the years.

Classroom of love
affirms my faith —
school of life

NOTES

1 Seng T'san, *The Book of Nothing: A Song of Enlightenment,* trans. Phillip Dunn and Peter Jourdan (Kansas City, MO: Andrews McMeel Publishing, 2002), 16.

2 David H. Rosen, *The Tao of Elvis* (San Diego: Harcourt, 2002). Two newly designed and illustrated editions, with new essays by Thomas Moore and Clarissa Pinkola Estés, were published for the 35th anniversary of Elvis's death: a deluxe, hand-bound edition (Pittsboro, NC: Rosenberry Books, 2012) and a subsequent paperback (Eugene, OR: Wipf & Stock Publishers, 2013).

6

Jackrabbit at Eastwood Junior High

Playing is as precious as jade
and helps us find our way back
to the beginning — the source.

DENG MING-DAO
Everyday Tao:
Living with Balance and Harmony

Coming from the cozy all-A's womb of Mrs Murphy's classroom, I was an innocent when I entered the "real world" of Eastwood Junior High School, with its ups and downs. The ups were that I thought I could do anything: dance (which I could do well, especially jitterbug); go out with Cathy, the most striking girl in the seventh grade (five-foot-eight inches, blond and fully developed); play football and basketball; be Elvis (echoing Paul McCartney's statement, "When we were kids growing up in Liverpool, all we ever wanted to be was Elvis Presley."[1]); and be popular like my sister Janet. The downs were hard to take: I lost the election for vice-president of the seventh grade, and I didn't make the football team (no wonder at five foot three inches, with size twelve feet). However, I did make the seventh grade basketball team, and my nickname "Jackrabbit" was fitting as I hopped down the court.

Cathy, to my amazement, accepted a dance date, though my head rested between her large breasts during slow dances, which I secretly loved. I donned black felt side burns and did my version of Elvis's "Hound Dog" in the seventh grade talent show. This led to girls, girls, girls: "You're so cute," "You're the greatest," and I received one marriage proposal.... One Saturday afternoon, the bright, short and cute Hazel, an only child who had a crush on me, appeared at my house with her parents. My parents and I joined them in the living room. After refreshments and small talk, her father let the bomb drop: "We'd like you to consider Hazel becoming a suitable wife for your son." My parents were as flabbergasted as I was. This led to a polite No. Despite winks, kisses blown my way, love notes, letters, and invitations to many parties and dances, I did not go out with Hazel.

I was friendly with everyone, rich and poor, black and white, religious and not. I had a lot of friends who were girls and that has remained true during my life. To paraphrase one of Leonard Cohen's songs: girls were exceptionally kind to me and me to them. These friendships are reflected in my Eastwood yearbook. Lynda wrote, "You're a real sweet guy, and I think one of the cutest in the school." Trudie wrote, "Too good to be forgotten," and Judy added, "I think you may be a better Elvis than anyone I know." Alice penned the words "Keep being yourself and everyone will like you," and Gail wrote "You're one of the nicest and cutest boys in school. Love ya." Judith said, "Stay as sweet and good as you are now. Love you," and Cathy signed, "In the golden chain of friendship, regard me as a link." I also had a number of guy friends like Joe, Roger, Nate, Bebo, Charlie, Manuel, Keith, and Jim. So I guess I was popular, yet it was my true self. Adolescence allows for the symbolic death of one's parental ego and the rebirth of one's real self. As Sosan said, "Returning to your true nature, spontaneity and essence are found."[2]

There was also the dark side … like secretly smoking cigarettes and those first, tentative attempts at sexuality. Once a classmate told me and two other guys that his sister, who was a year younger, would let us see and touch her developing breasts. One evening this transpired. Being an inaugural experience, it is burned into my memory. I'll never forget how she slowly unbuttoned her blouse and undid her first bra. There they were, small tangerine-sized breasts with erect nipples. I was so excited that I could not say a word.

Looking back on Junior High School, three teachers stand out. Mrs Gimbel taught seventh grade language arts and Mr Dinwiddie taught eighth grade science. Mrs Backlund was the instructor of eighth grade language arts and English. In her journalism class, I worked on our school newspaper, *The Eastwood Eagle*. I have remained interested in the subjects elucidated by these teachers. Indeed, my love of writing stems from that creative start with Mrs Backlund, who on reflection, reminds me of Mimi and Mrs Murphy.

In the seventh grade I had some difficulties, and even made some B's and C's, as well as a D one quarter. Mrs Gimbel wrote to my mother that she gave me a D in seventh grade language arts because I was, "…too playful, even though bright and clearly a leader." My mother and I met with Mrs Gimbel. By the end of the year

I earned an A and an award — so I can turn things around quickly! Because I could knuckle down, work hard and get good grades, I was also known as a smart kid among my peers.

WITH FATHER, EIGHTH GRADE

The eighth grade was a pivotal year. My sister had graduated and gone to Central High School. Hence I was free to be my authentic self, with no sibling rival. Again, Sosan's words validate my experience, "True nature is impartial; it has no causes or rules. With the mind in undivided unity, wisdom is radiated."[3]

Of course, the other side of wisdom is foolishness, which also characterized my pre-teens and my first year of being a teenager (I was a year younger than my classmates). Although I masturbated a lot, I also lifted weights, and the eighth grade was a year of accomplishment. Despite remaining a human jack-rabbit, I made the football team and lettered in it. My short stature didn't prevent me from making the eighth-grade basketball team, but I didn't get to play, which was disappointing. Nevertheless, I was undeterred. In practice and later in pick-up games, I remember my black friends Nate, Bebo, Charlie, and Manuel helping me to almost overcome the adage "White guys can't jump." I came inches away from dunking the ball, a feat that I'd accomplish later in high school.

I didn't have a steady girlfriend, but I was well-liked and always had dates to dances and parties. I was still a young kid attempting to act like my older counterparts. My hormones would not kick in fully until I was a freshman in high school. When they did blast into my system, I'd grow two inches in several places and begin to shave. So it would be on to Central High School, implying that Eastwood was a lower school. This is accurate in a way, since junior high school is one of the most difficult passages for American youth. High school is equally arduous, but for different reasons, and the stakes are higher!

Falling leaves—
content to jump
and jitterbug

NOTES

1 Patrick Higgins, *Before Elvis There Was Nothing* (New York: Carroll and Graf, 1994), 48.

2 Mu Soeng, *Trust in Mind: The Rebellion of Chinese Zen* (Somerville, MA: Wisdom Publications, 2004), 155.

3 Ibid., 167.

7

Wild and Tame at Central High School

Adolescence is a normal psychosis.

SIEGFRIED BERNFELD

When I entered Central High School, a huge old red brick building with two thousand students, I was only thirteen years old. Although a true freshman, I was short with large feet, and I felt overwhelmed. This was one time I was glad that my sister was at the same school. Still, it was a bit much when we ended up in the same biology class. I had done so well in eighth-grade science that I was placed in an advanced sophomore science class in which I was the only ninth grader. Talk about sibling rivalry! This time I used it to my advantage and ended up with a higher A grade than Janet.

My sister was beautiful, smart, a sorority member, and part of the homecoming queen's court. Because she was so popular, I had instant visibility as her bright and cute little brother. I let it get to my head, however, when I was rushed by the Acorns, an equivalent of a fraternity. I used my new credential as a member of the Acorns, got a little wild and set my sights on going out with Peggy Sue, a cute and petite brunette senior-varsity cheerleader with freckles. I bet my friend Roger that, at the next home basketball game, I'd ask her out at half-time. As with Cathy, this continued a pattern of asking out girls who seemed inaccessible. To my credit, I did dress well and was on the freshman football team (but I never played). I also practiced lowering my voice, so I that would sound older. To my utter amazement, after I introduced myself as DH and asked her if she wanted to go out after the game, she said Yes. I'd won, so Roger had to give me five dollars.

After the game, I was on my own. I asked Peggy Sue what she would like to do. She said that there was a party at Kevin's place and asked if I had a car. I said No, but told a white lie when I added, "I just got my learner's permit." Actually I'd never even driven a car before. I wouldn't be taking driver's education until the following year. Because she accepted what I said, she would have thought that I was fifteen. I recall that she had just turned eighteen. Peggy Sue then said, "Well, let's go."

When we got to her car, a 1947 Chevy with a stick shift, she asked, "Do you want to drive?"

I said, "Not now, maybe later." I was relieved to have gotten over that hurdle. Like the therapist that I would become later, I asked her a lot of questions: about a boyfriend ("not at the moment"), her favorite activities, classes, teachers, cheerleading, sports, etc. I just kept the questions coming. She liked talking about herself, as most people do. Arriving at Kevin's house, I raced around and opened the door for her. We did things like that in 1959.

The party was incredibly crowded, and we could barely walk around. Thank God I didn't see my sister, but she would have been with a different group of students. Kevin's parents were not at home: in fact, they were away on a trip. There was plenty of smoking cigarettes and drinking alcohol. I found out quickly that Peggy Sue liked booze, and she drank a lot of rum and Coke. I thought I had to join her, but I had never drunk hard liquor before! I didn't like the taste or effect. It made me light-headed, so I drank mine slowly. She easily had four drinks to my one.

By the time we left she was drunk! I then realized that maybe this was the reason she didn't have a boyfriend. Once outside, she grabbed and kissed me several times and said, "You drive." I helped her get in the passenger side, and then I got in to drive. Peggy Sue wanted to make out first. I thought that I could do that by instinct, plus the alcohol and new surge of hormones helped. She was wild, directing my hand to her breasts and between her legs. I thought again that I was in heaven, but actually it was hell! I asked her where she lived so that I could drive her home and then walk to my house, which was not too far away. She had given me the keys and I started the car, but I didn't know how to drive! I asked her how to shift gears, and she tried to tell me, but she was fading. Miraculously, the car lunged forward as I popped the clutch, and the car raced down the street in first gear.

Instantly Peggy Sue threw up all over and passed out. In my surprise and alarm, I swerved and lost control of the car. I accelerated, when I ought to have braked! The car lurched sharply to the right, crashed into a little wooden fence and stopped in somebody's front yard. Though I was upset, I remained clear-headed enough to take action. As the lights went on in the house, I quickly exited and moved Peggy Sue over into the driver's seat. Her purse was there, so I knew they could identify her and contact her parents. I didn't stay to see what happened at the scene.

At school I heard about Peggy Sue's accident. She was not allowed to drive anymore and was receiving treatment for her widely-known drinking problem. I assumed that Peggy Sue didn't tell her parents about me, because she would have gotten into more trouble. Or maybe she didn't remember who I was.

I laid low for a long time and never got around or close to her. This experience taught me that it's better to accept oneself and not pretend to be someone you are not. So I went from being daring, reckless and foolish to being tame, gentle and subdued. I was glad when Peggy Sue graduated, because I knew I'd be a more relaxed sophomore without her.

Near the end of my freshman year I met Rose Ann. She was also a cute and short brunette, but I got lost in her eyes. She had the eyes of a doe: dark pools of divinity, which fit with her religious upbringing and nature.

Over the summer I asked Rose Ann out, and it was an opposite experience to Peggy Sue. This time I was involved in a relationship that grew gently and took its time. Her parents inadvertently helped, especially her strict father, because they were over-protective with a 10:00 PM curfew. I invited her to a Saturday afternoon and evening party at Keith's house, and Rose Ann said Yes. Her parents usually didn't let her date, but because this was a chaperoned picnic, and it was light out most of the evening, she was allowed to go. Rose Ann was one of the sweetest and kindest girls I ever dated. We started going steady, and my desire for a better relationship was realized.

My sophomore year was quieter than most. I excelled in my classes: Latin, geometry, English, history, and driver's education. I was not involved in organized sports, but I continued to play basketball at the YMCA. Related, surely, to my wild side, I took ballet. It didn't take long for my mother to convince me that it was similar to weight lifting, which was true. It was actually much more enjoyable hoisting and holding a lot of lovely teenage girls.

I had a soothing and deep bond with Rose Ann, and the year flew by. Reflecting back on that year, it seems to have been a healing time that I needed: the surprise of my life was about to happen.

When the summer of 1960 began, I got my first real job, at McDonald's making milkshakes. Elvis was returning from the army, and he had just released "It's Now or Never," which would become his best-selling record.

After the storm
greener greens—
dogwood buds open

8

Go West Young Man, Even If You Don't Want To

To live is so startling, it leaves little time for anything else.

EMILY DICKINSON

One calm summer day, my mother announced that we were going to Kansas City to visit her mother and my aunt (her maternal grandmother had died). She said we were going on a two-week vacation, which sort of made sense: we did this most summers. A slight tremor took place inside me when I had to ask to leave my job at McDonald's, which I'd just started.

My mother packed up my three sisters, my brother and me, and we left my father in Springfield. After ten days in Kansas City, a large tremor occurred when my mother proclaimed that we were going farther west to see the Grand Canyon. I didn't want to go because of Rose Ann and my job, but those reasons fell on deaf ears. The unspoken truth was that my mother was taking us to Nevada. Then the earthquake happened in earnest.

One night in a motel, after Bill (age eleven), Marti (nine) and Nancy (seven) were asleep, my mother told Janet and me that she was going to divorce my father. Janet and I were shocked, and tears welled up in our eyes. My mother's plan, which came to pass, was to drive to Reno, stay at the Lazy A Guest Ranch, establish residency in Nevada, and get a divorce. Following that, she was going to take us to California to Pops and Moms, who had moved to Garden Grove in 1957.

The Grand Canyon was not wide or deep enough for all of our tears and grief. When we finally pulled into the Lazy A Guest Ranch, we knew we were going to be there for a long time … long enough for my mother to change our lives forever.

The Lazy A Guest Ranch was an eye-opener. The proprietor's only son, Lee, a good-looking nineteen-year-old, expressed interest in Janet. She returned his affections, and was thus content to stay there and spend a lot of time in her bikini out by the pool. My brother and little sisters played and swam every day. They seemed to adapt. I, like Bob Dylan, was "always chasing after something, anything that moved — anything that might lead me into some more lit place, some unknown land downriver."[1]

I spent a lot of time with Red, the cowboy, at the bunk house or helping him with irrigating the fields and rounding up cattle. He taught me to ride a horse, shoot a rifle in case I had to kill a rattlesnake, and gamble. He also finally taught me to drive a pickup truck with a stick shift, even though I still didn't have a driver's license. One night after midnight, I drove him, drunk from a bar in Reno, the ten miles back to the ranch.

Red hinted that I should date Dawn, an American Indian maid who, at twenty-three years old, was eight years older than I was. She was pretty but tough, five feet seven inches in height, with bright eyes and long dark hair in a single braid down her back. I enjoyed looking at her and often fantasized about being with her. I also saw her check me out. I'd grown taller (nearly six feet), and although slender, I was strong and weighed a hundred sixty-five pounds. One evening when the moon was full, I strolled off hand-in-hand with Dawn. My heart was racing, thinking that perhaps this was the night that I'd lose my virginity. We walked far into the horse pasture and kissed passionately several times. Then she threw me down in the tall grass, and we rolled around. She wanted to have sexual intercourse. This rough advance scared me, and the two horses that stood over us didn't help. I said No and ran back to my room. I felt torn, because I wanted her on the one hand, but on the other hand I'd never done that before. She was just too aggressive. Nevertheless, I felt sad and inadequate.

Perhaps my fear and intuitive No were protective: after all, I could have fathered a child! As with Peggy Sue, I subsequently avoided being around or alone with Dawn. Still, it felt good that she wanted me. It was a confidence booster in a time of great trauma and transition.

While at the Lazy A Guest Ranch, my mother was fascinated with the making of the film *The Misfits*. She took us to the Mapes Hotel in Reno to see Clark Gable and Marilyn Monroe leave the hotel on their way to Pyramid Lake. This movie, the last for both of these stars, was an uncanny parallel to what my mother was doing in Nevada. Arthur Miller wrote the screenplay for Marilyn as a gift, but their separation and divorce were underway.

After the divorce, my mother drove us to Moms and Pops in southern California. Garden Grove consisted of acres and acres of orange groves that were being subdivided. It was fun playing among the oranges, throwing and eating them. There were several advantages to staying with Moms and Pops: a stable home, warmth, generosity, and Disneyland was in nearby Anaheim. We got to go to this new and exciting amusement park several times. They bought us new wardrobes, since we had brought little with us. In my case, I'd outgrown everything! After three weeks, we headed north to the Santa Cruz area, where we rented a furnished house with an ocean view in lovely Aptos. It was terrific being by the beach, swimming and building sandcastles.

Then reality set in. School started, and Janet and I had to ride a school bus to huge Watsonville High School. This only lasted one day. I remember gangs chasing me and yelling "Get the new kid!" I wouldn't return, and Janet joined the protest. This led my mother to find and buy, with assistance from her father, a new house in Ben Lomond, California. Our house was in the beautiful San Lorenzo Valley, which has the Santa Cruz Mountains on both sides, with redwood forests and the San Lorenzo River running through it.

We had to make furniture, since we went from being rather well-off to relatively poor. We assembled dining and coffee tables out of large and medium-sized doors and wrought iron legs. We also made couches out of smaller doors and shorter legs, upolstering them with thick pieces of foam rubber. My mother was a talented seamstress and fashioned covers for the make-shift sofas. She also covered the left-over pieces of foam rubber to make pillows. Our living room was lined with unique couches, which could be used for sleepovers or guests.

As soon as we moved in, Janet and I started attending San Lorenzo Valley High School in Felton. We were, at least, welcomed into this much smaller high school of only three hundred students. In fact we made friends quickly, and Dan became my new best friend. The junior high and elementary schools were contiguous with the high school. After the thrill of getting my driver's license, I bought my first vehicle for a hundred dollars, a 1937 black Dodge pick-up truck. I was then able to drive all of us to school. Every weekday my mother, who now had to work as a social worker, went north over the Santa Cruz Mountains to the city of San José.

Empty new house —
smell of redwoods
sound of a river

NOTES

1 Bob Dylan, *Chronicles: Voume One* (New York: Simon & Schuster, 2004), 108.

9

Sorrow and Courage at San Lorenzo Valley High

When sorrow comes, let us accept it simply, as part of life. Let the heart be open to pain; let it be stretched by it.

A. POWELL DAVIES

Being the main man at age fifteen, as well as a pseudo-father figure, messed with my mind. I was depressed. Below the surface I was angry and felt guilty about it. One of the insights I've had in writing this memoir is that I was too close to Mother. This cast me as a mama's boy, which primed me for problems with women.

It's the ancient Oedipal complex: kill Father and marry Mother. The divorce led to that constellation. My mother had bad-mouthed our father, and we bought into it. Furthermore, without a father in the home, I tended to regress and act out. I revisited my wild side until I ran into authoritarian figures, such as the high school principal and the police. This is how juvenile delinquents are formed, but the spiritual core of my being and my resilient nature saved me from continuing down that path.

My first act of defiance was to put detergent in the town fountain in Felton one night, which made the local newspaper. In the morning it looked like it had snowed overnight! I also had a way of getting into trouble in classes for inattention, playfulness and passing notes to flirt with girls whom I thought were cute. I'd then be sent to Mr Johnson, the principal. Through no fault of his own, he looked a little like an ape. He punished me by making me sit and study for hours, in a room alone.

Going down a dark path, I got together with two other troublemakers, Pete and George. One night, we defaced the high school and specifically targeted Mr Johnson. Clearly, I had a negative father complex. I cut out cardboard shapes of ape footprints, and Pete took paint, tar and liquid steel from his father's workshop. George stole a wooden cross from a cemetery and painted over the name and dates in white. He added Mr Johnson's name with the dates of his birth and fictional untimely death the following day.

We all worked on the Johnson grave by spading fresh dirt in a long mound outside the picture window in his office. I stenciled ape footprints from Mr Johnson's office door to the girl's bathroom, up walls and off into the woods by the sports field. I also put liquid steel in the keyhole to Mr Seely, my chemistry teacher's, classroom door. Pete and George took buckets of different colored paints and poured some into drinking fountains. Then they painted the wooden picnic tables that were used at lunchtime. In addition, we put tar on the chain-link fence where students leaned to chat before school and during breaks between classes.

We were caught by the police and charged with vandalizing public property. George, who was an eighteen-year-old senior, had to spend a night in jail. However, the police took Pete and me to our respective parents. The police told our parents that we would be reported to the juvenile authorities. The juvenile authorities would contact them and the high school principal about how to proceed. What had started as a fun night turned scary. Even though it was after midnight, my mother invited the officer in for some hot chocolate. The policeman liked my mother and downplayed the seriousness of what we did, "Oh, boys will be boys." Because I'd never been in trouble with the police before, he thought it would be resolved at the school level.

The next day the damage was being done: kids got tar on their clothes, the drinking fountains were unusable and students laughed about Mr Johnson's footprints going to the girl's bathroom and up walls. Two students, who were helpers in the principal's office, saw his grave. They leaked the information, so the whole school knew about it. Lastly, Mr Seely's class had to wait outside his classroom because he couldn't get the key in the keyhole!

I'll never forget sitting in Mr Johnson's office and apologizing to him in front of my mother. It was one of the most embarrassing and humiliating moments of my life. The punishment was harsh, but fair and effective. In lieu of juvenile detention, we had to remove all painted footprints and tar. We also had to repaint all the picnic tables a natural brown color, buying the turpentine, acetone and paint ourselves. Thankfully, there were no records of our offenses after we did what was required. We had to do all this one hour before and after school and during all breaks between classes. This stipulation insured a proper dose of shame. We were also required to pay all cleaning bills turned in by students and all plumbing and locksmith charges. The cross had to be returned with an apology, and we had to pay for it to be professionally repainted. Because my mother refused to pay any of my expenses, which were considerable (she did loan me the money), I had to work.

Getting a job was a godsend. I started working in less than a week at Johnnie's Super Market in Boulder Creek, the next town up the valley. This job enabled me to pay my debts to my mother, which included a loan of a hundred dollars. It also gave me spending money and allowed me to save for a cool car to replace my old truck. I felt like a man, and it helped me develop responsibility. I made the varsity basketball team, and went to work after practice, so I worked late. Eventually Johnnie trusted me to close up the store. Working late and closing up allowed me to study and do homework most nights between customers.

I was so happy to be on the varsity basketball team, something I probably could not have done back at Central High. Although I was now six feet two inches tall and weighed on hundred seventy-five pounds, I rarely started a game, but I played a fair amount. In my eagerness to play, however, I was too rough on the court, so I made more fouls than points! I'm sure the football coach noted my nickname, Freight Train, since I was encouraged to try out for varsity football the following year. I even had a small cheering section that periodically chanted, "We want Freight Train! We want Freight Train!" Thank God for coaches and male teachers who became healthy substitute father figures.

Sniffles, a cute freshman pom-pom girl, caught my eye. She was attractive, but had a little larger than normal nose, which led to her nickname. I talked with her at school and liked her. Dan was dating Gina, another cute freshman pom-pom girl. He encouraged me to ask Sniffles out, so we could double date. Since Sniffles was going with Larry, a star of the junior varsity basketball team, I thought she'd say No. To my surprise, the pattern unfolded again, and she said Yes, and broke up with Larry. Eventually, Sniffles and I started going steady; we were infatuated with each other. Sniffles was sort of a combination of Rose Ann (sweet and kind) and Dawn (a bit too sexual).

By the spring of 1961, when I was sixteen and she was fourteen, Sniffles wanted to make love and get married. This led to our breakup, which I still feel a little heartbroken about. First "true" love or "puppy love" always seems hard to get over. We understood each other well, since both our mothers had divorced our fathers and taken us across the country.

Her father was a policeman in Florida. That, however, is where our stories differed. Her mother had remarried an unemployed alcoholic, who used to beat her and threaten Sniffles and her little brother. It was a tense, and at times frightening, household. I think that might have been the reason behind her wanting to get married at such a young age: to get out of a bad situation.

At any rate, I would not have sex with her, and marriage was out of the question. I wanted to make love, but I abstained from sexual intercourse out of fear of the unknown and what might happen, like getting her pregnant. In the face of my fear, what I decided to do was right. I was a messed-up teenager myself, and I intuitively knew that having sex with her would make it worse.

Several months after I broke up with her, Sniffles shot her stepfather. Her mother was at work, and her stepfather was drunk, threatening to hit her and her brother. She didn't kill him. She only wanted to injure him, which she did. Her mother subsequently filed for a divorce after Sniffles said, "It's either him or me." I can remember visiting Sniffles in juvenile detention, where she was held and evaluated for a short time. Her case was quickly ruled self-defense and, because she was a minor, psychotherapy was arranged to help her deal with her own wound.

I had another bout of wildness toward the end of my junior year when Sylvia threw a huge party, when her wealthy parents were away on a cruise. They had spoiled Sylvia, their only child, and trusted her at home alone. In California, there were cigarettes and marijuana to smoke and all kinds of alcohol and drugs to get high on. I got drunk and passed out on bourbon, which to this day I won't drink. I ended up being showered by Sylvia and woke up nude in her parents' bed while she was having sexual intercourse with Rat Man, a high school graduate and furnisher of booze and drugs to underage kids. I sensed that I was going to be next, so I jumped out of bed, found my clothes and ran home. I think this was another fortunate turn of events. I was waking up in more ways than one, and just in time!

Overall, my senior year was good. In the fall of 1961, I tried out and made the varsity football and basketball teams. I lettered in football and again in basketball. I also made the track team and lettered in it too. Once I placed fifth in the mile. I got to know and like a lovely young woman named Marÿke, a senior exchange student from Belgium. She was smart, tall at five feet eight inches, and attractive with short, sandy, blond hair. I ended up dating her and taking her to the senior prom. I even visited her in Europe, and we've remained lifelong friends.

GRADUATION FROM HIGH SCHOOL

My work at Johnnie's Super Market continued, and I made more money than the other employees. When President Kennedy got the minimum wage bill passed into law ($1.25 per hour!), I went to see Johnnie in his office. I said to him, "I'm sure you heard the news, and now I want the minimum wage instead of ninety-five cents an hour!" Johnnie said, "Okay, but don't tell the others." Soon I saved enough money to purchase a 1956 metallic blue Chevy convertible, with white tuck and roll upholstery. Cars were very important to us then, and I felt like I had entered the pearly gates.

Janet, who had graduated the year before, was Miss San Lorenzo Valley. She went on to attend the University of California in Santa Barbara. My mother continued to commute each day to San José, which meant she left before sunrise and got home usually after sunset. This caused me to become, during my senior year, even more of a surrogate parent. My brother Bill, at twelve years old, was often the oldest person at home after school. He and my younger sisters, Marti (ten) and Nancy (eight), rode the school bus home because I had after-school practices in one sport or another. Of course, when I didn't have practice, I drove them home and helped them as best I could. Theoretically, my brother looked after his little sisters until my mother got home from work. In fact, we were essentially without parental guidance for much of the time, which allowed for the joys and dangers of too much freedom.

Dan and I became friends for life. An affirmation of this was when, in 2002, we both attended our fortieth high school reunion, and our friendship was the same as it had always been. In high school, Dan's family became a second family to me. I really liked his mother, older sister and younger brother Chuck. I felt especially close to his father Milt, who was a surrogate father for me. He was tall, like I'd become (six foot four inches), gentle and kind. He didn't yell or argue, and if the kids were complaining about something like taking out the trash, he quietly did the task. A calamity involving Milt occurred after Dan and I graduated from high school in June 1962. However,

I wouldn't get the terrible news until three months later.

In dire need of a closer relationship with my father, over the summer I went back to Springfield to visit him. My father worked very hard and got up at the crack of dawn to perform surgery. We always had dinner out, and then later we would play chess or Scrabble. My father had a few whiskies every night. As boys do, I loved my father. Yet, emotionally, it was a distant relationship even though I was "at home." At the same time, I was so financially dependent on him that I was a dutiful son.

Having been afraid of having sexual intercourse, I took a chance when I was in Springfield and called Hazel. I used my father's Pinto station wagon and put a mattress in the back. I picked up Hazel, and we both lost our virginity at my family's farm. There were donkeys in the field at our family farm. I'll never forget how several of them looked in the window while we made love.

Later that summer, I traveled to New York City, where I spent a month with George Edgar, a wealthy middle-aged friend of my mother's who lived in Greenwich Village. He produced the play *The Blacks*. I met all the actors, including Maya Angelou and James Earl Jones, at a cast party held in his luxurious penthouse apartment. A critical initiation experience occurred when George left me in the care of Mara, one of his girlfriends, while he went to Southampton for the long Fourth-of-July weekend. Mara was a bright and beautiful thirty-two-year-old woman of medium height with short brown hair. She was very kind and loving and took me to interesting places that I had never gone to before.

When I flew home to San Francisco, prior to going to college at the University of Southern California, my mother picked me up. Once on the road heading for Ben Lomond, she said, "I have some bad news. Milt killed himself." I was stunned, but managed to ask, "How? Why?" She said, "He shot himself with a rifle on the front porch. Chuck found him when he came home from the first day of school." She didn't know why.

To this day, I still don't understand why. I remember the hopelessness of thinking to myself, that if Milt could kill himself anyone could, even I. Milt's suicide, the suicide of my poet friend Sam Thomas, as well as my own episode of suicidal despair[1] has led me to research this topic extensively.[2]

Now, like Camus and Shakespeare, I'm on the "to be" side, rather than the "not to be" side of this fundamental philosophical issue.

Glorious pink clouds
at sunset —
another one gone

NOTES

1 David H. Rosen, *Transforming Depression: Healing the Soul through Creativity* (York Beach, ME: Nicolas-Hays, 2002), xvii-xxii.

2 See *Transforming Depression*, 251 in the bibliography under Rosen, D.H. 1970, 1975, and 1976 a & b. Also see Rosen, D.H. "Transforming Depression Through Egocide," in *Sacred Sorrows: Embracing and Transforming Depression*, 198-213 (New York: Tarcher/Putman, 1996); Rosen, D.H. "Depression and Suicide," in *Open Questions in Analytical Psychology*, edited by Mary Ann Mattoon, 612-619 (Einsiedeln, Switzerland: Daimon Verlag, 1997).

10

Drop Out at USC: Drop In at Shimer College

You are the master of your life and death.
What you do is what you are.

LAO TZU
Hua Hu Ching, Verse 40,
trans. Brian Walker.

It states in the June 1962 high school graduation edition of *San Lorenzo Valley School News*, under "Future Plans" of the graduates, that "David Rosen will major in Civil Engineering at the University of Southern California (USC)."

Looking back on this intention, I now realize I wanted to be like Pops, who was a civil engineer. Furthermore, going to school there meant I'd be in Los Angeles, close to Moms and Pops. This made going from nowhere to somewhere a lot easier. Before my first day at USC for registration and orientation, I stayed a few days with Moms and Pops. I felt loved and confident as I embarked on what I thought would be the first step down the path of becoming a bridge builder.

After I checked into the dorm and met my roommate, I went out to buy my textbooks for calculus, physics, physical chemistry, etc. The texts were huge, heavy and unwelcoming. When I returned to my room, Peter, my preppy roommate who was pre-law, wanted to go to the fraternity rush parties.

Having nothing better to do, I went along with him. At each frat house, we were invited in and offered all kinds of booze. Members told us about the fraternity's history and why it was the best one to join. A key feature of each pitch was the exam files. Each solicitation emphasized that if you pledged with that fraternity, they would guarantee you an A average. To prove their point, and to my utter amazement, they asked what classes I was taking and showed me the examinations with all the questions and correct answers. There was also a lot of hype about the prestige of the university and all the athletic programs, especially their famous football team (some of the fraternities even guaranteed great seats!).

After only a week of classes, I became demoralized. I was put off by the immense size of USC (fourteen thousand students), the resources and energy pumped into the sports programs, and the fraternities with their shiny veneer covering excessive partying and cheating. Maybe I was naive, but I thought college would be different from high school. I thought a university would be about the exchange of original ideas, and that I'd learn how to think and create. I was disheartened by all these things and the huge classes, some with as many as four hundred students. I felt like a number instead of a unique person.

I also felt confused because I didn't like calculus, physics or physical chemistry. Then I simply realized that I was not civil engineering material. I loved Pops, but I was different. I requested and received a refund for my registration, dormitory fees and unused textbooks, and I dropped out of USC. This was another symbolic death and rebirth experience. I thought I was being courageous, but others, like my dad and Pops, thought I being was foolish.

Being truly lost—unintentionally this time—I embarked on the Herculean task of searching and finding an alternative. My father was always consistent: either you go to college, graduate school or professional school, and he would pay for it, or you get a job and you're on your own. Given such clear guidelines, I telephoned my favorite cousin Ken, who was the same age as I. He was so smart, getting eight hundred on both SAT exams, that hundreds of colleges and universities were offering him full scholarships. I had stayed with Ken after my parents divorced, and I loved him like a twin brother. He accepted an offer from Lehigh University, and he, too, was starting out in engineering. Ken, who could have been a therapist, listened to my lament. He recognized my predicament and the despair I felt. He asked, "What do you want in a school?" I said, "Small, no fraternities, no nationally impressive sports programs, and no textbooks." It sounded like a dream, but I continued, "I want to read original works and learn to think and write creatively." Ken thought a while and said, "I think I know the school." He said, "Let me call you back after I find the letter and brochure." In about forty minutes, Ken called back and said, "It's a small experimental college called Shimer in Mount Carroll, Illinois, supported by the Ford Foundation." It met all of my criteria, including no textbooks! Ken gave me the admission director's name and telephone number. I called him and explained my situation. He said, "If you got into USC, we'll accept you. I recommend that you visit, but come prepared. If you like it, stay." The timing was perfect. Shimer didn't start until the following week.

I sold my '56 Chevy and thus sacrificed my high school identity. Selling the car gave me spending money and helped me to become more independent from my father. Following tearful goodbyes to Moms and Pops, I got on a plane to Chicago with only two suitcases. I took a taxi to the station and rode the train due west to Mount Carroll, a small town in the middle of cornfields ten miles from the Mississippi River and the Iowa border.

Shimer College was quaint, and almost looked like a New England campus. I liked it, so I stayed. The little town had a bar, Poffy's, which I frequented. Poffy's did not have a problem serving alcohol to students, maybe because it was an economic boon. Shimer College was the total opposite of USC: miniscule (three hundred twenty-five students), no fraternities or sororities, and their English Composition class challenged us to write creatively. According to the *Harvard Educational Review*, Shimer was one of the eleven colleges in the United States with an "ideal intellectual climate."[1]

While I was a student there, on October 21, 1962, Aldous Huxley received an honorary doctorate degree. I met him at the president's house — one of the advantages of a tiny school. It's one thing to read *Brave New World*, but another to meet the author.

I wrote essays, poems, and even a short play. The curriculum at Shimer was modeled after the University of Chicago's "Great Books Program." For example, we actually read writings of Sigmund Freud, rather than a psychology textbook. We read Karl Marx's own work instead of a Political Science textbook. I had gotten what I wanted. In addition, Shimer had an intercollegiate basketball program. Basketball was my favorite sport, so I thought I'd died and gone to heaven. A benefactor, who also loved basketball, gave Shimer money with the proviso that they start a real basketball program. The school had a small gym, and the special gift allowed Shimer to obtain a state-of-the-art bus, uniforms, equipment, and an operating budget that included a salary for a coach and trainer. Coach Shepherd was known by everyone as Shep. He was a tall friendly fellow, with a red face and a crew cut. He had been working on a PhD in physical education for many years.

I was able to get a single room, which, being a basically introverted person, I liked. I had a girlfriend named Beth, who was a little like Rose Ann: a short and attractive brunette, who was kind, gentle and extremely smart. I also became good friends with Rich, Curt and several others who ended up with me on the basketball team.

When I tried out, I made the basketball team. But that's not saying much because anyone could have. It was perfect. Twelve tried out, twelve made it, and there were twelve uniforms! I realized that this was my chance to be a star. At the time I tried out, I didn't realize that Shep was a serious alcoholic. He had two strict training rules, which he told us about while puffing away on a cigarette: no smoking or drinking in the opposing team's locker room. These were really rules that Shep himself attempted to stick to, but he'd often whip out a flask of vodka and have a drink at half-time, even in the opposing team's locker room.

Of the twelve who made the team, only three had ever played high school basketball: Curt, Rich and myself. At six foot four inches I was the tallest, so I played center and started all the games. Shep's practices were regular but not very strenuous. He had only one play called "Rosie." Either Curt or Rich, who were the guards, would slap the ball and say "Rosie." The other guard would run over and block the man guarding me. I'd roll off the screen, receive a pass and shoot if I was open. It sounds ridiculously simple, but it enabled me to score up to twenty-three points in one game. For a nothing sports school, Shimer had a tough schedule that included playing against the University of Illinois at Chicago. At the opening jump ball for this game, I recall bearly reaching the armpit of the six foot eight black center. In that contest they quadrupled our score, 124 to 31!

Shep wanted his team (actually himself) to

"relax" before games. On the way to our first game against Dixon College, I remember my shock and disbelief when the bus driver, who knew the route and custom well, pulled into a tavern. When we entered Shep said, "Set 'em up for my boys. They've got their first big game in two hours!" The truth is indeed stranger than fiction.

On our way to a game with Aurora College in near blizzard conditions, we stayed too long at the bar de-stressing and unthawing. The home team was already on the court completing their warm-ups when we arrived. Exiting the bus, Curt passed out and fell in a snow bank. I remember Shep getting the trainer to give him oxygen and ammonia, while Shep slapped his face. Curt woke up and staggered into the big gym. Shep kept saying, "You'll be all right, Curt." Needless to say, he didn't start that game, but he did rally and play the second half.

At half-time against George Washington College in Chicago, we were only a point behind when Shep said, "We can win this one, and I'm not even going to have a drink." He reviewed our situation and for once gave us a real pep talk! Unfortunately, or fortunately, we lost that game.

The peak experience for our team and Shimer College occurred when we set a national record. The team carried Shep on its shoulders around the dining hall amid wild cheers. Shep held up the *Chicago Tribune* with his photo that documented the event. It showed Shep with a top hat and the number thirty-six stuck in the brim. Our national record was for the most consecutive losses by an intercollegiate basketball team.

During the following year, when I was attending the University of Copenhagen in Denmark, I read on the back page of the *New York Herald Tribune* that Shimer had set an international record at fifty-nine straight losses! I heard later that Shep was fired and took a job at a junior college in Alaska.

After my foray into intercollegiate basketball, it was back to serious study. Shimer was one of the best educational experiences of my life. However, the school proved to be too small and incestuous. It was a little Peyton Place! For instance, there was a beautiful female student who got an A in a class because she slept with her male professor. Another girl from California was kicked out for sexual promiscuity because she gave the same venereal disease to five guys. The doctor in the health clinic finally figured out what was going on.

An alarming sequence of events occurred when I went to New Orleans for my first college spring break. I answered a Chicago newspaper advertisement, "Driveaways to most Cities." The weird office in a bad part of Chicago ought to have tipped me off, but I innocently drove a stolen car across state lines from Illinois to Missouri and on to Arkansas and Texas. The plan was to drive to Longview, Texas, where the used car dealer would give me a bus ticket to New Orleans, as they had no driveaways direct to New Orleans. I thought it was a good deal. I would receive a hundred dollars and gas money, which would enable me to make a little money and get to New Orleans for nothing.

I called my father at seven on a Saturday evening from Saint Louis, Missouri, to tell him that I would get to his house, our old house on 900 East Walnut Street, in Springfield about midnight. When I arrived, the back door was locked. There was no porch light on at either the front entrance on Walnut Street or the side door on Dollison Street. I rang the doorbell and knocked at the Dollison entry. Finally, one light went on, and I could hear a gruff, "Who is it?" I said loudly, "Your son, David." My dad opened the door and behind the screen door he stood with a loaded rifle pointed at me!

Scared to death, I said, "It's me, your son." In a flash of sanity, he lowered the gun barrel and opened the screen door. Then, as if nothing had happened, he said, "Hi, come in." We walked into the kitchen, where he poured a water glass full of Yellowstone Whiskey and asked, "Would you like a drink?" I replied, "No, thanks." We chatted for a little while, and then I said I was tired and went to my old room to sleep. I said that we could talk at breakfast, which we did, before I left for Texas.

Soon after I crossed over the state line from Arkansas into Texas, I was arrested and handcuffed by the Texas Rangers. That's when I was shocked to learn that the car I was driving was stolen. Following a check on my identity, which included calls to my father and Shimer, I became a decoy for the Texas Rangers, who followed me at a safe distance to the used car dealer. Once I entered the office, they stormed in and arrested the owner and associates. The Texas Rangers said they were sorry and bought me a bus ticket to New Orleans. In addition, they gave me another hundred dollars for helping them out.

Despite the two traumatic events, I had a wonderful time in New Orleans. I explored Bourbon street, and I made a point to go to Preservation Hall, where Dixieland Jazz began over fifty years before! Having learned the hard way about driving to New Orleans, I went back to Chicago by bus and on to Mount Carroll by train.

My year-long education at Shimer College succeeded in whetting my appetite to travel and explore the world. Travel would become essential for knowing myself. Wole Soyinka put it this way, "The road and I thus became partners in the quest for an extended self-discovery."[2] A seed was planted. I wanted to see and experience the place where so much of Western culture originated.

With my parents' support, I applied to go to Greece for the summer and live with a family as part of The Experiment in International Living, which was established in 1932 to foster peace through understanding, communication and cooperation.

One door closes
another opens—
Hellenes calls

NOTES

1 George Stem, "Characteristics of the Intellectual Climate in College Environments," *Harvard Educational Review XXXIII* (1963): 5-41.

2 Wole Soyinka, *You Must Set Forth at Dawn: A Memoir* (New York: Random House, 2006), 47.

11

Greece: "Moments, Moments, That is Life"

Marvelous things happen to one in Greece

HENRY MILLER
The Colossus of Maroussi

I was pleased to be going to Greece and to partake in its venerable culture. As a participant in The Experiment in International Living, I felt like an ambassador, and it was an exciting time in my life. After an orientation at the headquarters in Putney, Vermont, which included an introduction to Greek customs and language, I departed for Greece with ten other college-aged Experimenters to spend the summer of 1963. It was a novel experience, an adventure to a new, yet ancient world. I had recently turned eighteen, old enough to vote and fight in a war. I felt free, independent and responsible.

Upon arrival at the Athens International Airport, we were met by our Greek families. Each family had a son or daughter who spoke English and became a brother or sister to the Experimenter. Alexander (Alex) Tritsibidas, who was my age, became my brother. We got along so well that our friendship has continued to this day. I have gone back to Greece to visit, and Alex has come to visit and live in the United States. In fact his first son, Spiros, was born in California. Neither Alex's sister Vicki, who was twelve, nor his parents knew English. So if Alex was not present I had to speak Greek. My host family had a very nice apartment in Athens, and a simple summer home in Kifissia where we spent most of our time. Kifissia, at the foot of Mount Pentelikon, was nine miles from the center of Athens and linked to it by an electric railway. Renowned for its exquisite climate and lovely gardens and parks, Kifissia was the birthplace of Menander, the greatest writer of comedy in the fourth century BCE. My task was to learn the language and to live as my family lived. I would also visit national museums, meet my country's ambassador to Greece and tour Greece.

I wholeheartedly recommend a book but with a caveat: if you read it, you'll probably be on your way to Greece! This is exactly what happened to me when I read *The Colossus of Maroussi* during my year at Shimer College. The book is about Henry Miller's experiences in Greece, when he found himself. Just as he describes in the book, I too found the Greek people to be enthusiastic, curious-minded, kind, generous, and passionate. I felt right at home with the following accounts of Miller's: "Everybody goes the wrong way, and everything is confused, chaotic, disorderly. But nobody is ever lost or hurt, nothing is stolen, no blows are exchanged"[1]; "The Greek…is an adventurer: he is reckless, adaptable, he makes friends easily"[2]; "The Greek way…is aimless, anarchic, thoroughly and discordantly human."[3]

During my second night in Athens, Alex and I walked through old Athens, the Plaka district, at the base of the Acropolis. The moon was full and Alex said, "Let's walk in the moonlight." We walked up Philopappus Hill to view the Acropolis, which was lit up with the Parthenon as its crown. I wrote in my journal: "Neither my words, nor anyone's, could describe the beauty of Athens by night. It has a special glow. I've seen many American cities at night, and San Francisco is only one-twentieth as beautiful. I imagine a photo would not capture what I saw. The only way to see and feel the beauty of Athens is to come here and experience it."

On our way back to Kifissia, Alex, who grew up learning about Socrates, Plato and Aristotle, talked about his philosophy of life. His philosophy was very simple: "Moments, moments, that is life." It is true and now I share the same philosophy.

Once a brother
always a brother —
blessed by two!

The house in Kifissia was in the country and had apricot, pear, pomegranate, and fig trees, a grape vineyard, as well as the ubiquitous olive trees. My family was rather traditional. My father *Patera*, a lawyer, was the head of the house, and *Mitera* was a superb mother, wife and cook. The first night she made lemon soup, a salad of tomatoes and cucumbers, and zucchini stuffed with lamb and rice. I had eaten everything, and I said in my newly-learned language "Thank you very much for the delicious meal." She said something quickly to Alex, who told me that his mother had conveyed that no words were necessary, as I had eaten everything on my plate.

Alex attended the University of Athens, which, to his credit, was very hard to get into. Each year around three thousand applied, but only three hundred got in. He was studying law, and eventually he took over his father's law offices in Athens. After his father died, he opened an office on the island of Paros, where he now lives. Alex was medium height and looked like a Greek god. He was sort of a playboy, and girls loved him. Often he arranged for two girls to go with us somewhere, like Lilian and Lina (a Swede and a Greek), who went with us one day to the isle of Salamis. We visited a monastery on the top of the hill. The nuns accepted Alex's big line about how we were reporters from *The New York Times* doing a story about their monastery, which would require interviews and photos. It felt wrong to lie, but it was relatively harmless, and besides, we had these girls on our minds. It turned out that lunch as well as a siesta was part of their kind response.

Among the Experimenters were Laura (Lolly) and her Greek sister Pola. I'd wanted to get to know Lolly because she was bright, beautiful and twenty. One evening, Alex invited Lolly and Pola to his family's charming but unoccupied apartment in Athens. We enjoyed dancing to Alex's favorite music, he particularly liked Nat King Cole and Johnny Mathis, and we attempted to break the ice by talking about Greek and American sex theories and practices. Of course, the slow dancing and kissing helped! I liked Lolly a lot, but she had a boyfriend back in America.

Often we spent our days at Vouliagmeni, south of Athens on the Saronic Gulf. It had one of the finest beaches for swimming in the area. The sea was a clear raspberry blue, and the sand was golden. Another day we had a humbling tour of the Acropolis. I wondered what would remain of our civilization when it was gone. The Greeks not only left impressive ruins, but also ideas and art that have shaped the whole of Western culture. Like many people at that time, I believed that our world would end in a nuclear holocaust, so I decided to enjoy the moment.

My Greek mother woke us up each morning by sprinkling drops of water on our faces. What a lovely way to be awakened into the new day! After a few minutes I was up walking about in the sun and cool breeze. I liked to begin the day by standing beside a fruit tree in the stillness of the garden. The smells of the morning were wonderful: hay and goats mixed with fragrant and pungent flowers. For breakfast, we had thick Greek yogurt with honey on top, bread and coffee. After a day and evening in the city, Alex and I would often return late. In darkness, the stars in the country were magnificent, so clear and bright. I thought, "No wonder astronomy flourished in ancient Greece with this panoramic night sky." No matter what time we got home, midnight or later, we were always met by Mitera's smile, hug, kiss on the cheek, and dinner.

After three weeks of settling into the Greek way of living, our Experimenter group embarked on a trip around the country. We visited the Peloponnese (Corinth, Patras, Pyrgos, Kalamata, Sparta, Tripoli, Argos, Mycenae, and Epidaurus), two Ionian islands (Zakynthos and Kefalonia), and Delphi. Of these places, I was taken with majestic Mycenae, its massive Lion Gate and walls made of gigantic stones. I was also impressed by spiritual Epidaurus where the healing temple of Asclepius, the Divine Physician, housed circular dream therapy chambers and an ampitheater. The incredibly huge theater is so well designed that, even in the most remote seats at the top, you can hear the whispered words of someone at center stage. However, my favorite sacred place was Delphi.

The drive from Patras was lazy. We then took a two and a half hour ferry boat ride across the Corinthian Sea. At Itea on the other side, we had a picnic of bread, cheese, tomatoes, watermelon, and cold water. We then started a bus ride, ascending steeply to the famed ruins of Delphi. It was a beautiful ride. You could look back on the tiny village of Itea far below and see the miniscule fishing boats in the deep blue sea. The mountains around Delphi are gray with cliffs soaring very high, some even sheer. The setting of Delphi is the most spectacular in Greece.

I experienced a pleasant surprise when my sister Janet came to Delphi from Israel, where she was part of the People to People Ambassadors Program. This organization was founded in 1956 to promote cultural understanding and world peace. After spending the night at Delphi, I got up very early at sunrise and had breakfast with Janet and Lolly. Then we headed down the path to the archaeological site. I was walking fast and soon left Lolly and Janet, who lagged behind talking. I wanted to be alone with my thoughts, walking through the pines with the sunlight dancing. I reflected, "What potential energy and creativity humans have! Just look at these remains of a civilization, which is beyond comparison to anything I've ever known."

I started climbing on a stone walkway past the Treasury of Athens. Then I turned a corner and ascended a rock staircase into the prodigious Temple of Apollo. The columns were unlike any I'd seen: very thick, tall and beautiful Ionic columns. The stone upon which the Pythia, the priestess of the oracle, sat had been removed from the temple and placed on display in the front. The stone had three holes where the stool legs used to reside, a fuming indentation and a shallow channel for the holy water, which was ever flowing. The Pythia could interprete codified messages from Apollo via the fumes if, for purification, she washed her lips and body in the holy water before and after receiving Apollo's word. The priests of Delphi would take the simple message and give it two interpretations, one good and one bad.

For a thousand years the Delphic Oracle played an active part in predicting outcomes of a vast array of problems, such as deciding on war or peace. A small narrow stairway led from the far rear corner of the temple to the Delphic theater. The view from the top row of the theater was especially rewarding. The columns of the Temple of Apollo contrasted with the soaring cliffs, which seemed to be reaching for the azure sky. The never-ending sight of olive groves and far-off mountains was striking. The patterns and colors of the green vineyards and terraced wheat fields made a pleasing combination. I climbed from the well-preserved stadium to the highest precipice I could reach. I could have stayed on that rock atop the cliff forever; inside was a feeling of deep peace and harmony. That kind of beauty, and the impact of this ancient home of gods and goddesses, touched my soul. I remained there for at least two hours. Far below, I could see the tourists milling about like ants.

After I left my imagined spiritual home, I went in search of the Castalian Spring, which I eventually found. I went up to the source and drank some of the pure cold water. I walked from the spring to *Marmaria,* the Sanctuary of Athena, and to the temple dedicated to Athena. In the afternoon, we went to the museum at Delphi, which houses one of Greece's best archeological sculptures, a bronze called "The Charioteer." I was sad when we left Delphi, as I felt I was leaving behind divine friends, unsurpassed beauty, and most of all, my refuge at the edge of the bluff. The ride from Delphi to Levadia was refreshing, as was our supper by the springs of Levadia, where my Greek father drove to get its special, virtuous water. We spent that night in a lovely park back in Kifissia, at Alaska Bar with Alex, Lolly and Janet.

About midway through my stay, I announced to Alex and my family that I wanted to go off on my own for three days to a remote fishing village somewhere with no access by road. My objective would be to see if I could make it on my own, utilizing the Greek I'd learned. I recall Arthur Miller's words from his autobiography, which also apply to me, "I kept riding into the future forever, practicing a defiant loneliness — that cousin of revolt — blindly groping for the beginning of the lifelong voyage toward myself."[4]

Alex suggested Sarandi because I could take buses to Hostia in the mountains by way of Thebes and Domvrena. He left me at the main Athens bus station after helping me get my tickets. I met a girl named Eva who was going to Domvrena to see her relatives. Going from Thebes toward Domvrena, we went through fertile land with cotton, rice, onions, vegetables, olives, wheat, and fruit. Domvrena is a small and beautiful village at the base of a mountain, whereas Hostia, where I'd spend the night, is at the top. Eva took me to visit her *Papous* (grandfather), who was ninety years old but looked seventy! Over an open fire he made us a lunch of spaghetti, goat cheese, tomatoes, and *Retzina*, a resin based wine. We had a brief siesta and *Papous* arranged a talk with the mayor. We toured the Domvrena church (the priest was so kind, his face seemed happy and at peace), school, jail, and more. To get to Hostia, I took another bus. The mayor of Domvrena gave me the name of the mayor of Hostia to help me find someone to stay with.

I ended up staying at George's three-room house with no bath ("go in the hills"), and no running water. George's wife and three-year-old son, his widowed mother, brother, and sister-in-law all lived there. Following a dinner of meat cooked in bitter unprocessed oil, cheese and lots of *Retzina* to drink, we discussed politics: Karamalis (the conservative President), *Ohi* (no); Papandreou (the liberal candidate who would become Prime Minister), *Malista* (yes); Eisenhower and Nixon, *Ohi* (no); Kennedy, *Malista* (yes).

I was happy that night, especially when I saw the ladder to the roof where I was to sleep. Overhead was a heavenly dome with bright stars. I had one of the best sleeps of my life!

The next day we were up with the sun. George got us two donkeys to go down the other side of the mountain to Sarandi, a jewel of a village in a pristine bay.I had accepted George's offer to accompany me there and back. Sarandi was tiny with only sixty inhabitants, all fishermen. George and I stayed with a kind and generous family, a young man Pedro and his wife Rina. They prepared fresh-grilled fish along with the potatoes and greens that George brought with us. There was more *Retzina* and lots of laughter.

The peak experience was spending the next full day out fishing at sea in Pedro's boat. We caught plenty, and George took a supply up to Hostia with us in the morning. Living a simple life hit home.

Impulsively, I decided that I'd become a fisherman, since I was good at it and thought that I would enjoy that way of life. After I returned to Athens, I was thrilled about my new vocation, so I told Alex and my family. I could see the shock on their faces. When I wrote to my father, he seemed to understand and accept my fate. He wrote back, "Congratulations! Good luck fishing and stay in touch!" I replied immediately that he should send money, as I had to buy a boat and have something to live on. Knowing my father, I also said that if I couldn't be a fisherman, I wanted to stay in Europe as a student. My dad answered, "I will only send you money if you go to a college or university," and, here's the catch, "where the credits you earn will transfer to an American college or university. Doing so will allow you to graduate with a bachelor's degree after four years."

In an era without computers, I set out to find such a school. Fortunately, through planning a farewell party for the Experiment in International Living with the US Embassy, I met Mr Alberti, the assistant to the US Ambassador to Greece. He was very kind and helpful. I learned that he graduated from the University of California, Berkeley, in International Relations and took the Foreign Service exam. Mr Alberti then took his current job with the US State Department. I expressed interest in his field and said that I'd like to stay in Europe to study. He mentioned an excellent program at the University of Copenhagen in International Relations, taught in English, with students from all over the world. I explored this possibility and found material about the program with the help of the librarian at the US Embassy. I applied when I read that credits from this program would transfer to Whittier College in California near where Moms and Pops lived. I got accepted to Whittier and the University of Copenhagen, and everyone was happy, including myself. I even arranged to live with a Danish family while going to school there.

Before we left Greece, the Experimenters were given five days for independent travel in Greece. Lolly and I decided to go to Rhodes. Going there by boat was an ordeal, as we were on deck in a storm. Thank God for a young Danish couple who shared extra raincoats with us. Each day we set out from our base, a hotel in Rhodes, and explored the island on our rented scooters. The first day we explored the dry, west side and ended up at the wondrous Acropolis of Lindos. On the way, we swam in the blue-green Mediterranean Sea and lay out on isolated and beautiful beaches. Often we were nude, to let the healing rays of the sun penetrate and transform our bodies. We were used to the hot Greek sun, and it was easy for both of us to become more golden. We headed back to Rhodes in the evening, struck by a full moon and how it seemed to affect our loving hearts. After a great meal and wine plus *ouzo*, we sort of slept. The next day we went to the wet, east side with its greenness, windmills and Petaloutha Valley. *Petaloutha* means butterflies, and they were everywhere. It was magical!

The memory that haunts me the most is of lying at night, naked, next to Lolly on our pushed-together single beds. Beads of sweat clung to our bronzed bodies like erotic dew and rolled down our sides like miniature silent streams. As Lolly kissed me many places, I would want to make love, but then I'd be moralistic, "No, you have a boyfriend." Lolly would back off, and I would start kissing her, tasting her salty moisture. Then she'd pull back and say, "No, I'm in a committed relationship." We'd lay there like that night after night, wanting each other more than anything. This is probably why Lolly is still one of my dearest and most talented friends: she paints, takes photos and writes beautifully.

Beads of
dewy friendship,
flowing forever

NOTES

1 Henry Miller, *The Colossus of Maroussi* (New York: New Directions, 1941), 15.

2 Ibid., 32.

3 Ibid., 39.

4 Arthur Miller, *Timebends: A Life* (London: Minerva, 1990), 63.

12

Athens to Copenhagen

For every traveler who has any taste of his own, the only useful guide book will be the one which he himself has written.

ALDOUS HUXLEY
Complete Essays: 1920-1925

Fall was approaching, I flew from Athens to Paris on my way to Copenhagen after tearful goodbyes to my Greek family. My first impression of Paris was that it was cold. After the enjoyable ninety degree temperatures of Athens, the fifty-four degrees at the Paris airport made me shiver. I met a guy named Don from California who had spent the summer in Iran. We went by bus and taxi to a hostel he knew about. It was the Catholic Students' House at 61 Rue Madame. For the equivalent of $3.60 per day, we received three simple meals and lodging. The Parisians seemed detached, busy, and unfriendly. There were exceptions, like students and small shopkeepers, who were unusually friendly and helpful.

Don and I were exhausted. After lunch, we slept through dinner and got up with the sun. Our first day in Paris was spent figuring out the metro system. We found the Opera House and headed for the American Express Company, directly opposite, to retrieve our mail.

From then on, we always rode in the first class car. The French are very class conscious and even the subway has classes! When the ticket lady came around for the special blue first class ticket, Don and I successfully feigned ignorance by speaking Persian and Greek, respectively. Soon she gave up, and we settled back into our comfortable cushioned seats. In Paris, we walked through the verdant Luxembourg Gardens, the amazing Sorbonne and the lovely Saint-Lazare Church of the Trinity. We also saw the impressive Montmartre, with its Place du Tertre (the painters' district) and the Eiffel Tower.

It was a beautiful sunny day and the temperature warmed to around sixty-five degrees. We met two French girls and sat with them on the bridge over the Seine River at the Institute of the Arts. We had both taken French in high school, so we spoke as best we could. As if in a dream, we gazed upon Notre Dame Cathedral and the river below. An American tourist stopped and asked us in broken French if he could take a picture of us on the famous bridge! We smiled, and a chorus of *Mercis* emerged. There we were, two guys from California who didn't look particularly French, with attractive, authentic Parisian girls. After the American was a safe distance away, we had a good laugh.

The next day I returned alone to two places I wanted to explore in more depth. Sacré Coeur (Sacred Heart) in the Montmartre district was the first. It was built in the nineteeth century and remains a colossal landmark in Paris. It looks sort of like a pure white Moslem mosque with its pointed domes. However, inside it was all Catholic with large murals, statues of the Virgin Mary, confessional booths, and nuns with baskets in their hands who said *Merci* after each coin was dropped in. It was a gigantic and beautiful church, but I preferred the smaller and simpler Saint Germain des Prés. The latter is the oldest church in Paris, built in the twelfth century, when there was only a meadow surrounding it.

Then, like most tourists, I visited the Eiffel Tower. It was amazing, and nearly everyone who goes to Paris visits it. I don't know what I was expecting, but that famous landmark was simply an enormous towering mass of steel! The gardens and grounds around the base were beautiful to walk through as I gazed up at the gigantic masterpiece of erector-set craftsmanship. The view from the top was remarkable. You could pick out the famous Parisian landmarks and appreciate the wondrous design of the city.

On the second level, I winked at a cute young blond woman, which later got me a date with her when we met again at American Express. Her name was Sue Tripp, a twenty-year-old flight attendant. She had won a car, boat, and a trip to Paris on "The Price is Right" television show. I called her up at the Grand Hotel and asked her if she would like to go to dinner and afterwards make a night of it at Les Folies Bergère. To my delight she said Yes! I went to pick her up, and the desk clerk said she was waiting in the bar. When I entered, I met Sue, her mother, and her mother's partner Buddy, a former president of some company. Buddy was in charge, and he asked what I wanted to drink. I replied, "A screwdriver." I listened to his stories and jokes and told a few of my own. Buddy ended up taking all of us to a dinner show at the upscale "Lido." Sue and I then spent time together and had a late night coffee. I walked her back to her hotel, where a parting kiss sealed a fun and memorable evening.

Anyone who knows me well realizes I am curious about many things. I have a deep-seated desire to understand complex individual and social issues. In Paris, I spent a fair amount of time in the Les Halles quarter, which housed markets for meat, poultry, fish, cheese, fruits, vegetables, and flowers. Les Halles bordered the red-light district with its sidewalk call girls, bistros, smells of all kinds, and very human people. Confronted by the riddle of prostitution, I decided to put into action the maxim, "Research is me-search." Walking around Les Halles, I was propositioned repeatedly. One time, in my accustomed style of moralism and fear, but with research in mind, I accepted and paid the twenty francs ($6). However, rather than partake in a sexual act, I interviewed the prostitute in an effort to understand why.

The streetwalker was a pretty twenty-year-old bleached blond with the saddest eyes I've ever seen. She took my hand and walked to a seedy hotel room that smelled of sperm and soap. I explained that I just wanted to talk. I asked her in broken French how and why she became a prostitute. Her cheap perfume and the cigarettes that she chain-smoked clashed like hail falling on an amusement park. She was painfully honest. At age fifteen, she was raped by her alcoholic mother's drunken boyfriend. She had an abortion and became suicidally depressed. Following this, she began to take drugs to dull the pain, which led her into prostitution.

By the end of the hour I felt deep sorrow, but I could tell that the young woman felt a bit better. Telling such a story allows for a little light to emerge from the darkness. Unknowingly, this woman was one of my early teachers. She prepared me for when, as a young psychiatrist and training candidate to become a Jungian analyst, a very bright young prostitute came to see me as a patient. To her credit, and thanks to the innate healing force of the psyche, she wanted to stop being a prostitute. In part because of my early experience, I was able to help this woman to face her wound of being sexually abused as a child and to transform her severe depression. She eventually became a therapist herself, working to help prevent and treat sexual abuse of children.

Streetwalker
tells her story—
Eiffel Tower pales

After spending quality time at the Louvre Museum, where I saw the *Winged Victory* statue from Greece and the *Mona Lisa* by Leonardo da Vinci, and the Rodin Museum, I took a train to Antwerp, Belgium, to visit my exchange student friend Marÿke and her family. Antwerp is a lovely city of fountains and many buildings designed in the eleventh to fourteenth centuries. There is an old castle, Ruben's paintings in the main Cathedral, and the Schelde River, which runs by Antwerp to the sea.

One day, Marÿke, with her teenage brother Remco, and I went to the medieval city of Brugge. During the thirteenth and fourteenth centuries, it was the most important commercial city in Europe, where the Flemish School of Art flourished. My memories of Brugge are of the windmills, the sweet brown beer made by monks, the walks through the narrow streets, and the old women making lace right before my eyes.

On another day, Marÿke's father drove us to his boat in Holland to go sailing. The lakes of Holland are about three feet below sea level, and the land is another three feet below the level of the lake. When you are sailing, this creates the illusion that the windmills, farm pastures, green fields, factories, churches, and trees are rising right out of the silvery water. The slowly turning windmills and plentiful sail boats contrast beautifully with the deep penetrating dark greens of the land and the white-gray bottomed puffy clouds.

Trees and windmills
emerge from water —
sailing in Holland

Leaving Antwerp for London, I was sad to leave Marÿke and her dear family. The trip from Ostende, Belgium, to Dover, England, was chilly and foggy, but two cups of tea helped. The White Cliffs of Dover seemed like a monument to Donne, the poet who wrote of them. At first they were a hazy gray and then brilliant white.

I met up with my Whittier College student group and toured London: Buckingham Palace and the changing of the guards, Saint Paul's Cathedral, Westminster Abbey, and the British Museum. At the British Museum, we saw the famed Magna Carta (circa 1215) and the Elgin Marbles, which include two pediments, fifteen metopes, and four hundred feet of frieze from the Parthenon. Lord Elgin bought all this from the Turks in 1820 for twenty thousand pounds. As a courteous and civilized act, I think Britain ought to return the Elgin Marbles to Greece. It is a shame that they have not been restored on the Parthenon at the Acropolis in Athens.

Our last night was spent in an English pub, the Watney Saloon of Jermyn Street. It was a friendly, family-oriented place, quite unlike our bars. It closed at 11:00 PM sharp. The next day we traveled on to Copenhagen.

13

Denmark: Society without Poverty

Early hath life's mighty question
thrilled within thy heart of youth
With a deep and strong beseeching
what and where is truth.

JOHN GREENLEAF WHITTIER
The Poetical Works of John Greenleaf Whittier

My Danish family was kind, but very different from my Greek family. Finn, the father, worked for the telephone company in the business office. Maddy was his American-born wife. They had two sons, Henrik (three) and Michael (five). We lived in a small but adequate apartment. Finn, like all Danes, was highly educated and spoke several languages. In fact, I can't recall anyone I met in Denmark, including bus drivers and waitresses, who didn't speak English. I slept in the living room on a sofa bed. Finn's parents were nice, yet reserved.

One day while taking a walk with Finn's father, I said Hello to a passerby, who said nothing in return. Surprised, I asked, "Why didn't that person reply and say something?" He answered, "We don't talk to strangers."

I was shocked, given my recent experience in Greece, where people spontaneously greeted each other with *Yasou*! Greeks would even go further and attempt to engage you in conversation. Although pleasant if they knew you, Danes were detached, depressed and even dour to strangers. However, shopkeepers and other workers were usually friendly. Again, I thought how different introverted Danes were from extraverted Greeks and Americans.

Given my adventurous style, soon after I arrived in Copenhagen, I used the excellent public transportation system of trams and buses and toured the city. The buildings, including the Opera House, theaters, churches, and castles (some still used by royalty, as Denmark is a constitutional monarchy), were beautiful, as were the many canals and parks.

Copenhagen appeared very civilized, and I saw no run-down or poor areas. As a result of my experience of urban areas in the United States, Athens, Paris, and London, I thought every city had its slums. In the poorest areas in Athens, the shacks were whitewashed, clean and often had flowers and plants in front. When I asked Finn and Maddy where the slums of Copenhagen were, they said that none existed. I was told that their absence was due to the socialist government. My eyes were opened to the idea that there was really no need for poverty, hunger, inadequate housing, or lack of health care. For the first time, I saw the immense value of a society that provided basic needs for all its people: welfare, health care (including contraception and dentistry), transportation, unwed mothers' homes, and education (including night schools for adults and the elderly).

There were also old people's villages, which incorporated daycare centers and after-school programs for children, thereby getting the young and old together for the benefit of both. Of course, the taxes were very high in Denmark, but they received many services in return.

Nevertheless, there was a downside to being too civilized. Denmark and other Scandinavian countries, and Switzerland as well, had very high rates of depression and suicide. After being shocked by Milt's suicide, I was so struck by the latter statistic that I decided to do an independent study researching Danish suicides. I wanted to discover why this problem was so common in this land of plenty. My project was a sociologically-based study that I wrote for one of my classes.

The very old homes had bubbled glass windows to ensure privacy; you couldn't see in, but you could see out. The old buildings, with their copper-plated towers that turned green when oxidized, contrasted sharply with new functionalist architecture imported from the United States and modern Europe. *Pølser* stands were scattered around the city. They served the Danish hot dog with spicy mustard and sweet ketchup. The Danish cheese and rye bread was also delicious, and I loved the flower stands and Copenhagen's walking street where no cars were allowed. Of Copenhagen's many photogenic organized parks, Tivoli Gardens was the jewel. Compared to other urban areas, Copenhagen was easily the cleanest city I'd ever visited.

Danes love to ride bikes. Finn, who bicycled to work, got me one. It was a joy to ride to the university and to go cycling with friends on the weekends. Denmark was so unlike the United States, where people felt that they must have cars and seemed embarrassed to ride bicycles.

SKETCH OF COPENHAGEN

In Denmark I grew a beard. Later I learned that depressed men often grow beards, so perhaps my melancholic nature was enhanced by living there. I started to smoke a pipe, a bad habit I had recently acquired, which may have been another symptom of increased depression. I was depressed because I was alone and away from my home, family and friends. Yet this introverted culture rubbed off on me, and my suffering was somewhat tempered by the educated and civilized society.

Finn took me to my first opera. How wonderful! The Danes grow up going to opera and theater. Finn asked me how I enjoyed certain scenes. It was embarrassing to be an American at such times because I often didn't know what he was talking about. I realized how uncultured Americans were and decided that I had a lot of catching up to do.

My classes at the University of Copenhagen were outstanding. They included Danish (required), International Relations (selected, as I thought I wanted to pursue a career in the Foreign Service), Art and Architecture (required), and Independent Study (I had decided to research Danish suicides). Sadly, my Danish class was not reinforced, since

Danes wanted to speak English. Danish, based on German, is guttural and sort of coughed when spoken, the embarrassment of which decreased the likelihood of my speaking it. Hence, I only remember two words: *hyggeligt*, which means cozy, and *æblekage med fløde*, which is a fairly good cream cake and fruit dessert that my Danish grandmother made.

My Art and Architecture course was elucidating and illuminating. Having started sketching in Greece, I continued to do so in Denmark, and many of my drawings were of things that impressed me from this class. We took many field trips to see various architectural styles: Romanesque, which is heavy and rounded with paintings on the walls; Gothic, with its verticality inside and flying buttresses outside, symbolizing the resurrection; and Reformation, when the Lutherans took over and whitewashed the wall paintings. We went to the village of Måløv and visited a church on top of a hill, a site where ancient Nordic people worshipped their gods. The church was built in the twelfth century and was originally Catholic. It had wall paintings depicting Biblical stories, high windows so people couldn't look out, and a flat ceiling. Between 1160 and 1260 about two thousand Romanesque churches were built in Denmark.

In Copenhagen we went to Rosklide Cathedral, burial place of Danish kings and queens, which was a little like Westminster Abbey in London. Patterned after French Gothic Cathedrals, it was started in the twelfth century and finished in 1350. We saw many tombs and statues of former royalty: Queen Margaret (1425), King Christian I (1449), King Frederick IV (1699), and King Christian IX (1905).

One day, I climbed round and round the same winding circular tower that Peter the Great once rode up on horseback. At a hundred fourteen feet high, the view from atop the Round Tower is impressive. I saw many buildings, churches and palaces built by King Christian IV.

Riding my bike on a sunny autumn day, I spotted some old women with folded newspapers on their heads for hats. They were sitting on old crates across from the canal bridge. I got off and walked my bicycle over and saw that they were selling fish and eels. The slimy eels were still alive and squirming around. The ladies used ragged gunny sacks as gloves in order to skin the eels and fish. I watched their hands flash over the eels. It took about a minute per eel! A statue of a fish market lady was erected close by.

From the sea—
old women deliver
fish and eels

A peak experience was my visit to Kronberg at Helsingør, which was depicted by Shakespeare as Hamlet's castle. It was huge, with fantastic green copper spirals and a grand courtyard. The whole castle was protected with moats and ramparts. I also immensely enjoyed my time at the Louisana Museum, which housed many of van Gogh's paintings. His work was so alive and full of color. There was even a sketch of the beautiful cathedral in Antwerp, which I'd seen when visiting Marÿke.

In my International Relations Class, we had a guest lecture by the Danish Minister of Foreign Affairs. It was an inspiring talk on the virtues of socialism and how the United Nations could evolve to be the center of a world democratic socialist government. I thought what a great way to effectively end war and put the resources used to kill people into helping everyone in our global village. Could we thrive and finally know peace … or was that utopian and unrealistic?

On November 14, 1963, my class was invited to McCormick Blair's home for a reception. He was the United States Ambassador to Denmark appointed by President Kennedy. Mr Blair was a lawyer who went with Adlai Stevenson when he visited Albert Schweitzer in Africa. His house was like a movie set, and he was married to a former model. Mr Blair had a fabulous library, which included books of Leonardo da Vinci's life's work. He also had signed photos of every President back to Fillmore, including three photos personally signed to him from President Kennedy.

He loved Greece as much as I. I talked with him about trips I would take, first to Berlin, in a week for four days, and then to the Soviet Union, via Sweden and Finland, for two weeks in December. He encouraged my interest in traveling and international relations.

On November 22, 1963, the world stood still with shock when President Kennedy was assassinated. I was in Berlin, and West as well as East Berliners openly wept. Candlelight vigils were held on both sides of the wall. This experience, coupled with my meeting Ruth Spiess in East Berlin, changed my view of people who lived under the Soviet sphere of influence.

I was walking down Karl Marx Alle, when I asked a professional-looking passerby if it was true that East Germans were oppressed and lived a horrible life. The woman responded in English, "No, we live a good life. I am a tourist guide and my husband is an economist and government official." Then, to my surprise, Ruth invited me into her home, a beautiful flat on the main street in East Berlin. I befriended her family. This friendship lasted, and I would return to East Germany to visit the Spiess family with my first wife during the summer of 1965.

As part of Nature—
every person
deserves a chance

14

To Russia with Love: Twist and Shout!

The use of traveling is to regulate imagination by reality, and instead of thinking how things may be, to see them.

SAMUEL JOHNSON
from Hester Lynch Piozzi's
Anecdotes of the Late Samuel Johnson, LL.D. During the Last Twenty Years of His Life

The year was 1951, and I was a second grader just beginning my path in education. One day my teacher distributed some pictures of a man's full face. I can remember her words, "This is Joseph Stalin, the cruel and hateful leader of the Russian people. He is mean and he hates America. Color him black, and when you go home show your parents and then tear it up and throw it away." I have never forgotten this. From that time on, by absorbing American propaganda, I began to distrust Russians, both the people and their form of government. I feared communism (although I didn't know what it was) and the Soviet Union because I was made to believe it was evil.[1] I began to imagine a country of cruel, larger-than-life communists who made slaves of the people. I envisioned the Soviet Union as a large prison with the Communist Party acting as the warden.

When I was a junior in high school and taking a comparative government course, I chose the Soviet Union for my topic. I wrote to the Russian delegate at the United Nations and the Russian Embassy in Washington, DC. At this time I began forming another idea of what the Soviet Union was like, based on propaganda from the other side. The pamphlets and books I received from the Russian United Nations delegate dealt mainly with how successful the Soviet Union had been with their five-year plans (for example, the Sputnik program).

I started a subscription to *USSR Magazine*. It showed and explained only the good side of Soviet life: smiling and happy workers and collective farmers; free medical and old-age care; education at no cost; the great industries of the Soviet Union; and their superb music and drama.

The two opposing visions of the Soviet Union I had formed in my mind raised several obvious questions. How could the Russians assert that their citizens were so well off if it was an oppressive dictatorship? Perhaps the American propaganda was false. Maybe Russia was a prosperous egalitarian land. Confused about the situation in the Soviet Union, I had a burning desire to see the truth for myself, but I thought that it was impossible to go to Russia. It was so far away, and there were logistical problems related to traveling there.I gave up the idea until the winter of 1963, when I found myself in Denmark and not that far away from Russia. Around mid-December, I decided to go to the Soviet Union on a Scandinavian student tour, which was leaving Copenhagen December 26.

The day following Christmas found me busy packing and very excited: I was going to the Soviet Union! The preceding week was hectic. I went to the Russian Embassy and the United States Embassy. At the latter, I received a most interesting booklet entitled, "So you're going to Russia!" One of the suggestions was: "Develop a direct, natural and relaxed approach to the people you meet. This characteristic is one of the great natural advantages of the American character. Capitalize on it whenever you can!"

After a last-minute check of the things in my suitcase and a mental note of my passport and ticket, I exchanged warm goodbyes with my Danish parents. I was off! I peddled my bicycle down the dimly-lit streets toward the railroad station. It was cold and damp on the ride there. My train was to leave around midnight, but I arrived at the station at eleven that night. I checked in at the Scandinavian Student Tour office and received information on the exact departure time and place.

Upon leaving Copenhagen by train, I began to rehash some of my impressions of what the Soviet Union was going to be like. On the one hand, I thought it would be a police state with communists in charge, and the people would be suffering due to a lack of freedom. I thought about the Cuban missile crisis, then just a year old; the tension in Berlin; the Hungarian revolution; and American propaganda. I also tried to imagine the other side: Russia as a land of opportunity, equality, and communism at its best. With a sigh of relief that I would soon be on the inside of that so-called "Iron Curtain," my eyes slowly closed.

My sleep was interrupted only by an hour-long ferry ride across the Baltic Sea to Sweden. Then we transferred to a new modern Swedish train, in which second class is like first class in any other country. Soon after leaving the station I was again asleep, not to awaken until the next morning as we were coming into Stockholm.

I started out my day in Stockholm with breakfast at the home of Carolina, a Swedish girl who was part of our group. Later she gave me a short tour of the king's palace, city hall and so on. Stockholm, known as the "floating city" or "Venice of the North", was one of the most beautiful cities I had ever seen. It seemed afloat with many inter-connecting isles. The modern freeways and skyscrapers contrasted markedly with the old town and its historic buildings, churches and quaint narrow streets. Some of the streets in the old part were so attenuated that you could touch both sides at once. It was a unique city, in and out of water, with a combination of rolling hills and winding streets. Stockholm had no slums, and I was stunned by its aesthetic.

By early evening, we were on our way by boat to Turku, Finland. The dinner on the boat was Swedish smorgasbord: about six kinds of herring, four kinds of fried and cooked fish, crab, and every kind of sardine; potatoes, vegetables and assorted salads; pork, roast beef, corned beef, chicken, and beer — all for $1.25.

We arrived early the next morning. Abo-turku was a desolate town with lots of factories, new apartment houses and a harbor. Black smoke billowed from stacks against the dark blue sky. Everywhere we looked were drab houses and apartment buildings: TV antennas on every one. There was some snow on the roofs but not much on the ground. An occasional soaring church steeple broke the monotony of the gray dullness.

As we headed toward the Finnish capital of Helsinki, thin dark-green pines stood out against the white snow on the rising hills. In Finland, I noticed some American influences: Shell oil, Coca-Cola, Chevrolet cars, and advertisements for Vicks' cough drops, among other things. I remember passing little red cottages tucked back among the snow-covered birches and pines. As we neared Helsinki, I wondered if Marja would meet me at the station as she had promised.

Marja was a very nice Finnish exchange student, whom I met in Washington, DC early in June 1963. We had been writing to each other, and I looked forward to seeing her.

She was at the station; blond hair, blue eyes and all. She invited me to come to her house for dinner, so off we went. It was an hour bus ride, but we talked the whole time about her experiences in, and impressions of, the United States.

Her house was simple, with a sauna bath house in the backyard. It was quite cozy inside, with a wood-burning stove and a Christmas tree. Before dinner I was to have a sauna with her father. I went out to the bath house with him. First, we took off all our clothes. Then we went in this really hot little room with wooden benches and a stove. The stove had red hot stones in it, and he poured water over the stones. We beat each other all over with birch branches to increase perspiration. We took this extreme temperature for about fifteen minutes. The cold shower afterwards was invigorating. I got dressed, but Marja's father wrapped a towel around his mid-section and walked barefooted in the snow to the main house, steaming like a hot lobster.

Then we ate a Finnish dinner that her mother had prepared: ham, red beets, carrot-apple-pickle salad with cream, herring, mashed sweet potatoes with syrup, raisins and rice, hot liver paste, and rice pudding for dessert. No wonder the Finns are so healthy with their saunas and delicious, wholesome food.

The next morning, Marja gave me a quick walking tour of Helsinki: the Olympic Stadium, the main Lutheran cathedral, the university, and the downtown section. At the Helsinki railroad station, I purchased numerous Western magazines (mostly American), to go along with the four cartons of American cigarettes and three and a half pints of Canadian Club I had bought on the boat. I waved goodbye to Marja and thanked her for her hospitality. It was noon when I left for Leningrad on a Soviet train.

The student tour group had grown, from a mere twelve that started in Copenhagen, to fifty-two upon leaving Helsinki. There were Germans, French, Swedes, Finns, Italians, Danes, Australians, British, Iranians, Americans, and a Canadian.

The young man from Canada brought a portable record player with him and one record. Yes, one record, which I must have heard over a thousand times! It was “Twist and Shout” by the Beatles. Along with wine and cognac, this made for a tremendous amount of boisterous twisting and chaos in the aisles.

We stopped at the Finnish border station to have our passports checked. We were there for thirty minutes, so the twisters assembled outside on the platform and the Beatles started to sing. Asses started flashing, faces were smiling, and the twisting was in full force. The Finns stood around with astonished looks on their faces.

Soon we crossed the border and headed for Vyborg, the Soviet frontier station.

Leaving Finland
twisting and shouting
our way to Russia

I glanced out the window and saw a white winter wonderland. With the Beatles still blaring, I wondered how many groups of students twist their way to Leningrad.

I had arranged for a two-person cabin with Robynn, an American student in the University of Copenhagen program. Robynn was short and real cute, with light brown hair. She was smart and witty.

The Russian trains did not have dining cars. However, a man came around serving tea, biscuits and cookies for a very low price. The tea was superb. It was served in large steaming hot glasses in polished brass holders.

Outside it looked like a Christmas scene. The pines had a blanket of snow at their feet.

We stopped very soon after we entered the Soviet Union at a border station, so that three customs officials could get on. They wore fur hats and long floppy coats and had strong lean faces. I asked, “How are you?” in Russian, to one of them, but he could not understand my version of his language. However, the superior officer understood and responded. He checked our passports, comparing my bearded face to my unbearded picture. “Please show your

American dollars. Do you have Russian money?" They stamped our passports, and we were free to leave the train during our thirty-minute stop.

When we entered the restaurant in the train station, we saw a fifteen-foot Christmas tree in the middle of the dining area. Our first Russian meal at the Vyborg station consisted of red fish, two kinds of bread, hot beef, red beets, and potatoes; with sugared rolls and Russian coffee for dessert. The station at Vyborg was crowded with people, poor and rich.

Soon after we left Vyborg, the porter returned and made up two bunks. Although never close before, Robynn and I talked and laughed together. Soon we were both in the upper berth telling stories and looking out at the barren white Soviet countryside. We rapidly transformed into the Rodin sculpture of two lovers: two yet one. We moved slowly in sync with the sound of the train. We fell asleep as one, but awoke as two to a knock before sunrise, which indicated that tea had arrived.

Making love
all night long —
clickety clack, clickety clack

NOTES

1 This lasted well into the 1980s. President Reagan called the Soviet Union an "Evil Empire". Of course, that all changed. The thaw began when Reagan held hands with Gorbachev during a walk through a forest in Iceland. They became lifelong friends.

15

The Soviet Union: Making New Friends

I cannot forecast to you the action of Russia. It is a riddle wrapped in a mystery inside an enigma.

WINSTON CHURCHILL
"The Russian Enigma,"
October 1, 1939 BBC broadcast

Before dawn, we pulled into Leningrad (now again called Saint Petersburg). There were neon lights, lots of trains, and many kinds of people, including Russian, Mongolian and Chinese. In the train station, we gazed up at a twenty-foot statue of Lenin and the ceiling mural of the October Revolution.

We were met by two Intourist governmental guides, Lily and Lena, and brought to the October Hotel. There were a few chandeliers, red carpets and long halls. The ceilings were twelve to thirteen feet high. The bathrooms offered hot rusty water and old toilet fixtures, but they served their purpose. The stiff, heavy toilet paper could also be used as stationery, wax paper or other things. The rooms were furnished to a minimum with a telephone, a shoe-shine kit and good heat.

I took out a map of Leningrad and looked at its size. It was a vast city. I considered all of the things I wanted to see in three days — impossible! Leningrad, being the second biggest city in Russia, was also the largest, northernmost city in the world, with a population that exceeded three million.

That morning, we took a bus tour of the city. The day was cold, gray, overcast, and as drab as the city. I saw many of the same type of green army trucks, but few cars and no capitalistic advertisements — it's funny how I missed their lively colors. Elderly women were selling tangerines on street corners. There were many Christmas trees, actually New Year trees: in Communist Russia, they celebrated only the coming of the New Year.

We started down Leningrad's main thoroughfare and busiest street at the Admiralty. We passed the Kazan Cathedral, which is also the site of the Museum of the History of Religion and Atheism. On the way, Lily, the guide, answered two questions. To "How many active churches does Leningrad have?" she replied, "We have fifteen Russian Orthodox, one mosque, one synagogue, one Baptist, and one Catholic." Asked "How do you celebrate New Year's Eve?" she answered, "We just drink vodka and champagne and have a good time."

We passed through an old residential section

on the Kirov Islands, where the big beautiful houses of the ex-nobility were now sanatoriums and old-age homes. Next, we came to the Kirov Stadium near the Neva River that flows into the Gulf of Finland. We ventured down to walk on the frozen sea, passing seated fishermen who had cut holes in the ice. On the way back to the hotel, we saw darling Russian children bundled up in their fur coats and hats, red mittens, and boots.

Both our guides were intelligent, and thought and expressed themselves well in English. Lily had a Midwest accent. She was short with black hair and had a young-looking face with dimples. Lena was taller and heavy set. She spoke like someone from Brooklyn.

Over lunch they addressed my questions with alacrity. Lily: "Yes, we have on reserve every American magazine in our libraries." Lena: "However, you have to have special permission to look at them. You have to be a scholar or scientist." Lily: "The majority of the people don't believe in God. I don't believe in God myself, but it's difficult to say why not." Lena: "She is an agnostic." We all laughed. Lena: "All of the young people are atheists because Marx and Lenin proved that there was no God." I brought up President Kennedy's assassination. Lily: "I was shocked and sympathized with the American people." Lena: "I thought if they could kill their own president, then they could kill anybody." Regarding Communism, Lily said, "We have what we need: home, clothing and food, but at times I dream of owning nylon blouses and skirts."

That evening I went walking on my own. In the windows, I saw decorated New Year trees and an occasional scene with Old Man Winter, who is comparable to our Santa Claus. I passed the Moscow Train Station and then a hat store, optical shop, grocery store, and candy store. The stores were crowded, since this was the last day before the holidays. The sidewalks were jammed, but I began communicating with two small boys, about eight and ten years of age. They were dressed in long coats and floppy fur hats. We entered a shop, where I ended up buying two sets of beautiful hand-carved *shakhmaty* (chess) sets. When we left, I gave each of the boys a pack of chewing gum, but they did not know what it was. I put one of the striped fruit sticks into my mouth. They did likewise. "Mmmm. *Dobre* (good)."

We then went into a bookstore where they bought me a poster of the recent Soviet women cosmonauts in space, as well as a picture postcard of Lenin as a child. One of the posters I bought depicted the Statue of Liberty with a sad face. She was shedding a large bloody tear that contained the scene of a black person being beaten by policemen. Later, I was stopped by a man who said he was a university professor, and I gave him copies of *Time* and *Scientific American.*

The next day, December 31, I teamed up with Robynn. We went to the Hermitage Museum, built in the eighteenth century for a czar. It was a spectacle: there was gold trim on everything inside, white marble columns, a red and green marble staircase, and huge chandeliers. The section on Western European art included paintings by Leonardo da Vinci, Van Dyck, Rubens, Michelangelo, Titian, and Rembrandt.

On my own at night, I could not find bars as such, but the liquor stores allowed the sampling of beverages for a nominal fee. I purchased two bottles of champagne for approximately five dollars. For another dollar, I purchased some caviar, bread and cheese. On my way back to the hotel, I encountered three female pre-med students, who took me to a fun New Year's Eve party.

Through Intourist, I secured a ticket to a late-morning performance of the *Nutcracker Suite* Ballet. I took a taxi to the Kirov Theater and paid the driver with a pack of cigarettes. The whole performance was fabulous: the story, the dancers, the music, the children, and the scenery.

I met Albert between the second and third acts by offering him an American cigarette. He thanked me and asked, in extremely broken English, where I was from. I said, "America, California." He said that he had been taking English for only six weeks, but he hoped to learn to speak it very well soon. I told him that what an opportunity it was to be inside a Russian home and actually visit with a family. I said slowly, "Can I go with you to your house to see your Mama and Papa?" He was very quick with a *Da* and then a Yes. I smiled and said, "*Da,* that is good." We agreed to meet in the lobby after the performance.

Albert introduced me to his eleven-year-old sister, and we started off toward their home. The paint on their yellow, but rather depressing, apartment building was peeling. In the basement hallway, the walls were filthy, and there was trash and dirt covering the walkway. We went upstairs to the third floor. Each floor had the same plan: four rooms (one family to each), two common kitchens and one common bathroom. Fresh paint was needed everywhere in the building.

I met Albert's father, mother and two grandmothers. During the next three hours, I spoke the international language of understanding, as well as hundreds of *Da*'s and *Spasibo*'s. An English-Russian dictionary also helped considerably. Albert said his mother would prepare food for us.

I scanned the extremely clean room. The television was on with an ice-skating show direct from Moscow. Above his parents' bed were Albert's father's and mother's portraits. The father's was in full military uniform with five medals on his chest.

I learned that he was a physician and surgeon, but earned only three thousand roubles, under four thousand dollars per year! He was also a Communist Party member and had been for twenty-seven years. As he wished, I called him Papa. I presented him with a bottle of Canadian Club whiskey and several packs of Pall Malls, which luckily I had brought along. Papa was one big *Spasibo*. He opened the bottle and conveyed that it smelled good. He unwrapped the cigarettes and immediately smoked one. Then with Albert's help, I learned that he was given some American cigarettes from a friendly American soldier, when the Allies met in Berlin during WW II.

I asked them about Kennedy, and they said Kennedy and Khrushchev talked and were making the USA and the USSR friends. They added that this was good because both wanted peace. His parents said they watched Kennedy's funeral on television and were saddened by his death. Papa got out the vodka and filled three water glasses. He and Albert each downed theirs in two gulps, and after each gulp sniffed coarse brown bread, a custom in Russia. It took me a sip and three gulps, which brought laughs because it had reminded them of Kennedy's vodka encounter when he met Khrushchev.

Now the food started to come in full force. All of it was delicious. There was a salad of potatoes, peas, mustard, egg, meat, and mayonnaise, a soup of chicken and rice, along with sardines, cheese, bread and butter, salami, fish, stuffed peppers, jelled cold meat, wieners, mashed potatoes, carrots and red cabbage. Then there were cookies and cakes, sugared blueberries and strawberries, two more kinds of cakes, and hot tea.

I saw with amazement how all of them could live in that one room, and my eyes were opened to the true nature of life in the Soviet Union. It seemed so small by our standards, but perhaps to them it meant a great deal, just the fact of having their own room to themselves. I explored the rest of the living accommodations. The kitchen was primitive, with ancient gas stoves, no refrigerator, but a lot of storage space. Shiny, spotless pans were hung on the wall above the stove.

They presented me with a pack of Papa's Russian cigarettes, a picture of a cosmonaut and a small statue of Lenin. I also received, from Albert's little sister, two small porcelain dogs and four pieces of candy to take to my two younger sisters. I exchanged ties with Albert. He received an Ivy League special, and I was given a plastic clip-on Soviet tie. Albert brought out his accordion and played while we had tea. I said goodbye to the family, and they thanked me for the gifts. I bestowed many *Spasibos* upon them for their gifts, the wonderful food and the whole experience. We shook hands and hugged.

Albert and I left for the Kazan Cathedral,

which focused on corruption in the church and its people, proving to Albert that there was no God. Soon Albert and I parted. We embraced and thanked one another. We vowed to write to each other, which we did for several years. Then we took subways in different directions.

As I came out of the subway station, I saw a beer stall across the street and a line of workers waiting to purchase beer on tap. I went over and offered some of the workers a cigarette. I soon emptied two packs. However, each time I gave away an American cigarette, I received a Russian cigarette in return. A worker bought me a beer, and I drank with the group for a while. They kidded me about my beard by calling me Castro.

It was around ten at night when I left the beer drinkers. I walked down the quiet brick street. The outsides of the apartment buildings still had bullet holes from WW II and were in dire need of repair and paint.

As I was venturing back toward the hotel, I came to the Anichkov Bridge, which has the famous four carved horses on each side. I encountered a Russian soldier in full uniform, about twenty years old, leaning over the rail and gazing at the frozen canal below. I offered him a cigarette and asked him where the October Hotel was. Taking me for a German, he replied in German. I said, "I'm an American, *Nyet* 'Germanica.'" We shook hands and smiled.

I understood, as he pulled me his way, that he would take me to the hotel. On the way we developed a system of communication: a thumb turned down meant *bad*, and a thumb extended upward meant *good*. The conversation contained only proper names and *Da*'s and *Nyet*'s. We both disliked Stalin. He liked Kennedy and was saddened by his death. He clasped my hand and said, "Kennedy and Khrushchev." Squeezing my hand, he said "America and Russia for peace and friendship in the world." I said, "*Da*, no more bang, bang," as I imitated sounds of war. He agreed! Upon reaching the hotel, I brought down a *Time Magazine* and some cigarettes. We parted as friends shaking hands again and hugging.

The student tour group departed on a 10:45

AM flight for Moscow. As the twin jet engines warmed up, I looked out at the snow-covered runway. The CCCP (USSR) on the wing looked odd, as did the Aeroflot inscriptions on everything. The jet roared down the runway and up and up, through the clouds and above them. The seats were comfortable, and it was a fast ride. Another piece of red candy from the stewardess, and we started to descend to the Moscow International Airport.

After lunch, we had a tour of Moscow by bus. The tour guide was very humorous. As we passed the public Olympic-sized, open-air, heated swimming pool that was filled to capacity with fun-loving people, she said, "This was specially arranged for American tourists!"

We went down Gorky, Moscow's main street, past the Institute of Marxism-Leninism and the guide added,"This may or may not be of interest or importance to you." We passed the Revolution Museum (now the State Museum of Contemporary Russian History), Pushkin Square, Chekov's House, and the Kremlin, which was a beautiful sight with the golden domes of the cathedrals reflecting the setting sunlight.

After the tour, I went over to the GUM Department Store on Red Square, the largest department store in the world. It had a fascinating variety of consumer goods. It was also very crowded. I bought a few things and continued to look in the school supply department.

I was locating San Francisco on a globe when a voice from behind asked, "Find your home city?" "Yes, San Francisco," I replied as I turned around. A tall young man named John was standing there. He was about twenty and had black hair, a large nose and black-rimmed glasses. He was casually dressed, except for a big bushy Russian bear fur hat. He said quietly, "I want to meet you later. I want a hundred dollars for one hundred-fifty roubles." We arranged to meet the following night.

The next day our group toured the largest ball-bearing factory in Europe, which manufactured fifteen hundred different types. We met with the director of the plant, his assistant and the Young Communist leader. I started a conversation with the leader of the Young

Communists. We talked, but slowly, since his English was limited and my Russian was almost non-existent. I said, "American tourists come to Russia to visit, and they find a strong country and good people." I paused, "In ten or twenty years, you will be a director in management." He smiled, and I continued, "And you will have many roubles. You come to America and see. We are good people and a strong nation, too!" He said, "Yes, I want to come to America." I said, "When you have the money to come you can visit me. We will exchange letters. That's good." He said, "Yes, yes." He gave me his Young Communist Secretariat pin and clasped my hand. I said "*Spasibo*." His face was glowing as we parted.

In the afternoon, we visited the University of Moscow in the Lenin Hills (now Sparrow Hills) District. It is huge, with thirty thousand students. It is meaningful that the tallest building in the Soviet Union is this university. We went through the main doors and down the hallway to the large main lecture hall. There were beautiful chandeliers, and on the stage were four columns with a prodigious mosaic behind them of red flags, banners, hammer and sickles. In the center of the mosaic was a fifteen-foot diameter picture of Lenin. Around the hall there were pillars and plants in the windows. Red velvet banners with gold lettering hung on either side of the end columns. The guide translated, "Communism establishes for the world: Peace, labor, equal rights, and happiness for all the people."

Later that afternoon, I visited the United States Embassy. I was informed that there were thirty-five Americans studying at the University of Moscow in a variety of fields. I asked an attaché at the Embassy how many people were in favor of the government. He replied, "Now it fluctuates, but we figure usually between fifty and sixty percent. However, in time of war it is ninety-nine percent." At the Embassy, I received two copies of *Amerika Magazine*, which was published in Russian for distribution in the major cities.

Before dinner, I stopped at the four-story children's department store across from our hotel. I asked at the book counter if they had any books by American or English authors. On display, they had a small selection of English copies of John Steinbeck's *The Red Pony* and works by Edgar Allan Poe and Jules Verne. In Russian translation, they had Ernest Hemmingway's *Old Man and the Sea* and Mark Twain's classics.

I took my new friend Robynn to see *The Snow Maiden* at the Bolshoi Theater that night. The inside was absolutely beautiful, and the main chandelier was glowing with crystals that sparkled in many colors. There were several balconies, and the whole theater was finished in gold.

The seats, drapes and trim were covered in scarlet velvet. The gold and red curtain was embellished with waving red banners, scenes of the revolution, the ubiquitous image of Lenin, and a hammer-and-sickle design that alternated with five-pointed stars. Greek goddesses graced the ceiling, and the gold decoration became Baroque in style over the main exit. Built in 1856, the theater still contained the Czar's boxes, rippling with red velvet drapes and elaborately trimmed in gold.

Both the performance and the set design of *The Snow Maiden* and were exceptional. I escorted my date outside after the opera. As agreed, John was in front of the theater. He said, "Follow me." He walked away briskly, and we followed him through the park in front of the theater. Across the street, we picked up his accomplice, another tall young man. John had on his large fur hat. We walked down Marx Prospect to the first street and then turned left, all the time talking. I said, "I have only fifty dollars in cash; that's all I could scrape up. I'll trade you for eighty-five roubles."

He thought for a while and consulted his friend for advice. John said all they had with them was seventy roubles. I said, "It's either eighty-five roubles or the fur hat and fifty roubles. As we walked, he talked it over with his friend and said, "All right." We approached a dark dimly-lit side street and John said, "Turn left and get your money ready." I started to stop and he said, "Keep walking."

After about two minutes we stopped, and he slowly handed me fifty roubles, all wadded up, as we shook hands. He said, "Count it." I said, "I trust you." As we resumed our slow pace, I pulled out my wallet and forked over fifty dollars. "Count it." He replied, "I believe you." John removed his Russian bear fur hat and placed it upon my head. We agreed to meet again the next day.

In the morning, our group visited the Kremlin, and the first stop was the Armory Chamber. It is now a museum and contains the former Czar's and Czarina's royal possessions. We next visited the Kremlin's three cathedrals: the Archangel, the Annunciation and the Assumption. The rare ornamental icons and frescoes in these churches depicted stories of their Christian heritage. These century-old cathedrals had been the bustling implicit centers of the so-called New Jerusalem.

We strolled by the new Palace of Congresses, where the Supreme Soviet sits. I left the group and headed for the candy-striped onion towers of the Saint Basil's Cathedral, an architectural miracle. Three separate churches are joined together, built as a monument to Ivan the Terrible's victory over the Tartars.

I then ventured from Saint Basil's down Red Square toward a huge solid red granite structure where Lenin lies entombed. He was preserved in a glass case, looking exactly as he did when he died in 1924. Inside the tomb, there was a religious and reverential hush in the air. Outside, military guards and fresh flowers adorned the mausoleum.

On the way back to the hotel, I got my best shoe shine ever. The man knew some English: "I got 'broder' in Chicago. He shines shoes too. He capitalist. I capitalist; I own my own stand. I make good money, and someday, I go to Chicago and work with my broder."

At the appointed 1:00 PM, John was in the hotel lobby. We went up to my room. He had brought a splendidly painted icon of a scene with the Virgin Mary and Jesus to trade for some clothes, but I just wanted to talk with him. I learned that he was a journalism student at Moscow University, worked for *Pravda*, and was "a Jew, not a Russian. You see, I don't want to be a Russian under the present government." I asked, "Why do you work for *Pravda* then?" John replied, "Because it is the best newspaper we have, and it is excellent experience. I seek to become a foreign correspondent for this paper, and I hope to get an assignment in America or Western Europe."

We then discussed the world political situation. John predicted that in the next war the US and the USSR would be allies a third time, but this time they would be fighting the Chinese. He seemed to feel that our two countries were drifting toward the same end, a sort of democratic socialism. We also discussed American writers. His favorites were Ernest Hemmingway and J.D. Salinger.

Subsequently, I went to the Communist Chinese bookstore. I purchased several books of prints and some Chinese folk tales, poems and stories in English published in Peking (Beijing). I spent my next two hours in the Lenin Museum. It was hard to fathom four entire floors filled with Lenin's articles, letters, books, furniture, clothes, and personal belongings. In every available spot and corner, there were busts, paintings, pictures, and statues of him.

Later that evening, I went to the Bolshoi Theater one last time to see *Sleeping Beauty*. The two leads in the ballet were extraordinary. The way they moved their bodies to the music was perfection in motion and timing.

I went back to my hotel room, took a hot bath in red rusty water, wrote a few letters, and made some notes in my diary. Then, about one o'clock in the morning, I ventured out with sketch book in hand and walked down Karl Marx Prospect, turned left past the domineering Hotel Moscow, then up to Red Square. The main Kremlin entrance tower has the most beautiful bells in the world, and they chime every quarter hour. As I slowly walked across Red Square, the Kremlin bells tolled, and I noticed the cold wet mist settling on my face. Some black birds fluttered silently through the dark violet moonlit sky.

A group of young students, who had evidently done some heavy drinking, were hollering and laughing as they strolled drunkenly along on the ancient red bricks. I went over and sat down on the concrete bleachers, which they use on days of celebration such as May Day, and started to sketch the Lenin Mausoleum and Saint Basil's Cathedral. A guard approached me and motioned for me to move on, which I did without hesitation.

I went gift shopping in the morning. I headed after lunch to a vast park in the suburbs to view the Exhibition of Achievements of the National Economy. I inadvertently got off the bus about a mile and a half too soon and walked through some of Moscow's slums. A young male student who spoke English escorted me to the park, but it took me another hour to find the main entrance to the exhibition. Since it was late, I saw only two exhibits: the Soviet Sputniks at the Space Pavilion and a graphic arts exhibit at the United States canopy. As I was leaving, I asked a young woman with her boyfriend where there was a metro station. She said, "Why, come along, we are going to take the metro."

SKETCH OF LENIN'S TOMB

The woman, an English teacher from near the Ukrainian border, said, "Pure communism in twenty years will be in existence in the USSR." She believed it! I said, "No war." She said, "No! No more wars!" I asked her about the Sino-Soviet inner-party troubles, and she said, "The Chinese are our friends, naturally." I asked her why they didn't sell the *New York Times* or *Life Magazine* in Moscow and why they had only one type of newspaper. She said, "We have newspapers from all over the world, and we can buy a New York paper or a French paper if we want to." She did not mention that those papers were the communist newspapers from these countries, that is, *The New York Daily Worker* and *L'Humanité*. Regarding the ubiquitous posters and propaganda, she said, "I've become accustomed to it."

I spent my last night in Moscow by myself, walking through the city. I encountered no one as I wandered alone with my thoughts, reflecting on the contrast between the government and the people of this nation. Crossing the Moscow River, I stopped in the middle of the bridge to gaze at the Kremlin. It was stunning at night with its huge glowing six-foot tall red stars atop the old Kremlin towers. The upward spirals of the central golden belfry tower gleamed.

Our group left for Helsinki at eleven thirty at night. On the way back, there were four people to a sleeping compartment and hot tea served within an hour after leaving. I started reading *The New York Daily Worker*, which I had bought in the Moscow Hotel. The feature article was headlined "Cuba's Fifth Year: Time for Friendship." Overly tired, I was soon fast asleep as was Robynn in her upper bunk.

As the sun rose, we were still traveling across the Soviet Union. More tea and cookies were served at around nine o'clock that morning. The train rumbled along at a fast clip. At 11:50 AM I felt a sense of relief as I looked out at the Finnish customs house. A mere twenty minutes ago, the Russian Customs officials had been ravaging through my luggage, searching, looking, feeling, asking, pausing, and reading my materials. The only thing that they frowned upon was a copy of the West German anti-communist newspaper *Posov*, which I had forgotten to give to some Russian. They thoroughly examined my Communist Chinese folk stories and paintings. They searched our cabin and our luggage more than any other cabin. I wondered why; what might they be looking for?

Arriving in Helsinki, I was met again by

Marja. After eating at a restaurant, we took in a French movie with Finnish and Swedish subtitles. I was so tired that I fell asleep.

The next day, we went by train from Helsinki to the coast and again crossed by boat from Abo-turku to Stockholm. The train pulled into Copenhagen Station around one in the morning on January 9. It was drizzling and cold as I wearily peddled home on my bicycle with two suitcases in hand and packages stuffed inside my coat.

Finn and Maddy were up with hot chocolate and cakes. Finn helped me in with my things. As soon as I took my coat off and sat down, I was bombarded with questions. What was your impression of Russia? What are the students like? Did you talk with many of the people? Are the people allowed to read western newspapers and books? Is there really a black market? How was the Bolshoi Ballet and Opera? Do the people like and approve of the present government? Is there any chance of a revolt?

I reflected for a moment, then shared my thoughts with Finn and Maddy. Culturally, the Soviet Union was more advanced than the United States. The Russian people have long held a great appreciation and respect for art, theater, opera, ballet, and classical music. Music and art appreciation are taught in the early grades. Hundreds of boys and girls might attend a given opera or ballet performance.

But the Soviet Union was less modern than I had anticipated. Their scientific advancement seemed confined to space technology, engineering, communication, and to a lesser extent, medical research. The Russian people, like human beings everywhere, were friendly and wanted peace, not war.

The authorities were attempting to create a perfect Communist State that would eventually mold everyone into an ideal Soviet citizen. I believe that such efforts will always be thwarted by the individualism inherent in human beings and that Russia's totalitarian state was already weakening. The influx of foreign ideas, customs and money was making Russians eager to venture beyond their borders. However, none of us could have anticipated

15 The Soviet Union: Making New Friends

Gorbachev, Yeltsin and the dismantling of communism in the Soviet Union.

Behind the iron curtain —
a lot of good people,
new friends

16

Returning to America and Facing Death

Death puts life into perspective.

attributed to
RALPH WALDO EMERSON

After six months in Europe, it was wonderful to reconnect with my family and experience freedom. I was also in culture shock: face to face with rampant materialism and poverty.

Before I left, I naively thought that the United States of America was the best country in the world. Coming back, I knew that other nations, like the numerous children in a large family, were equally valid and meaningful. I even contemplated, albeit briefly, immigrating to Greece. I'd enjoyed living with my Greek family and experiencing the egalitarian warmth and chaos of that country.

I also admired my Danish family and learned firsthand the benefits of democratic socialism. I had overcame my fear of communism and ventured into the Soviet Union, thereby realizing that there were good people everywhere.

In the countries I visited, I appreciated how essential the arts and culture were for people and their souls. I recognized how kind, fair and humane it was, as in Denmark and Sweden, to provide everyone basic needs: shelter, safety, education, health care, and a job or means of economic support.

On my way to Whittier College, I visited my father in Springfield, Missouri, and my mother, brother and sisters in Ben Lomond, California. Both were joyful reunions. I received another warm homecoming at Moms and Pops, prior to attending Whittier College. Although I was living in a dormitory at Whittier, I spent my initial weekends with Moms and Pops. We ate delicious meals, which often included Mom's homemade apple pie with vanilla ice cream. I still remember the touching conversations and intellectually challenging discussions concerning national and international politics. Dear Pops supported, while I opposed, the ultra-conservative Barry Goldwater for President. Pops also disputed my idealistic views supporting democratic socialism and the United Nations.

Donald, my Whittier College roommate, and I were very compatible. One day, when sitting and talking in the quad, a strikingly beautiful and graceful woman walked by. I asked him, "Who's that?" He answered, "Lynn; she's a graduating senior and a theater major. She gets the leading roles in all the plays." Donald could tell I was interested in her, so he said, "But don't get any ideas about dating her, as she's unavailable. She's engaged to be married this June to a guy named Phil, who graduated last year and now works as a reporter for CBS." It was as though he had thrown down the gauntlet, and I picked it up.

I liked all my classes: Introduction to Psychology, Russian History and Politics, International Relations, American Politics, Introductory Piano, and Golf (for Physical Education). After only a few weeks of a new beginning, tragedy struck.

I was at Moms and Pops, and we'd just finished our long Sunday meal. Pops was resting in his chair.[1] I went to the guest bedroom and was lying down and reading a class assignment. All of a sudden I heard Moms screaming, and I ran out into the living room. Moms was yelling and crying, "Pops is dead! Pops won't respond!" I checked and saw him slumped in his orange chair, cold and blue. I sadly agreed. Pops wouldn't respond and seemed dead. I told her to call 911, which she did, and within minutes police and firemen were at the house. They too concluded the same thing: our beloved Pops was dead, and it happened right under my nose. It seemed like I held Moms for hours, and we both cried and cried. The tears wouldn't stop.

It was so hard to call my mother. When I told her, she was silent for a long time, something I'd never experienced with her. Finally, she said that she and my brother and sisters would drive down as soon as possible. It was February 8, 1964. Pops had suddenly died of a massive heart attack at the age of seventy-five.

A photo taken the day of the funeral shows my mother's devastated expression. Pops' death had been a crushing blow for her. It also changed my life and was one of the reasons I shifted my studies to pre-medicine. I wished that I'd been able to do something to save his life. I felt badly that I didn't even know CPR, which I quickly learned. I got certified within weeks of Pops' death.

Over the next few weeks, I was grief-stricken and even went to a psychiatrist, who helpfully

GRIEVING AT POPS' DEATH

explained that grief was natural and that I'd gradually recover, which did happen. My nineteenth birthday,February 25, 1964, catalyzed a rebirth. Looking back, I can see that I began to incorporate some of Pops' immense strength, courage, humor, optimism, and determination.

Instead of becoming a civil engineer, I decided to become a healer and allow my gentle loving character to emerge. As I moved out of darkness into light, I made three life-changing decisions. I applied to transfer and was accepted to the University of California in Berkeley to study premedicine. I tried out and got the part of the Mayor in the musical *Bye Bye Birdie* so I could meet Lynn, who had the leading role in this musical. I also applied for a summer work-study program through the University of Washington in Seattle, where I was accepted and assigned to work in the new Oregon State Correctional Facility in Salem. The latter became a seed for my growing interest in psychology and psychiatry.

Scent of spring
her tulips
open

On the set of *Bye Bye Birdie*, I made a habit of asking Lynn if I could help her. She was receptive, and I'd get her snacks and coffee. Finally, I got up the courage to ask her out. Following the pattern, she accepted, to my utter surprise. On our first date, we dined out. We progressed slowly to movies and strolls on the beach alone. We discussed kissing — I was as yet unaware of Rumi's ancient wisdom: "I would love to kiss you. The price of kissing is your life"[2] — Lynn then broke off her engagement with Phil[3] and went with me to Seattle and Salem.

Two other noteworthy events occurred while I was at Whittier College. Lynn and I led a protest march advocating Civil Rights from the college to Whittier's City Hall, and Richard Nixon (an alumni of Whittier) donated an electric organ to the Quaker Chapel. He actually came to the college to dedicate and play it!

Across the room,
chair where my grandfather died —
autumn chill

NOTES

1 Moms gave me the chair that Pops died in, and it's in the living room of our home in Oregon. I wrote the haiku at the end of this chapter in the autumn of 2004.

2 Coleman Barks, trans., with John Moyne et al., *The Essential Rumi* (San Francisco: HarperSanFrancisco, 1995), 37.

3 To Phil's credit, he phoned me and told me, "Don't get involved with her. She'll do the same thing to you because she did it to another guy when I met her last year." I thought he was angry, which he had every right to be, so I didn't listen, and that was a big mistake. That experience, however, became part of my character. All wisdom evolves out of suffering, when its inherent meaning is discovered.

17

Working in Prison and Playing House

Working in prisons, I get to see the results of "bad" karma up close, although it's hardly any different outside the prison walls.

JON KABAT-ZINN
Wherever You Go, There You Are: Mindfulness Meditation in Everyday Life

Being young and romantic, I didn't realize that prison was symbolic of marriage, medicine, and academia — things I had decided to hasten toward, albeit unconsciously. In a real way, I was commencing the construction of a psychic prison that would take many decades to leave. I didn't realize the truth of Allen Wheelis' words, "If you weren't in a Nazi concentration camp, you'll put yourself in one."[1]

The beginning of the summer of 1964 found Lynn and me in Seattle where I had an orientation to the WICHE (Western Inter-Collegiate Higher Education) Summer Work-Study Program at the University of Washington. It was mid-June and an absolutely beautiful time in Seattle. Seattle reminded me of Stockholm because it is situated on peninsulas and islands, and it also seemed to be floating. In addition, Seattle valued culture and the arts.

Initially, I had hoped to be assigned to a facility in or around Seattle, but I was placed at a prison for first-time felony offenders in the capitol of Oregon. On the drive to Salem, we saw Mount Hood from the road as we skirted Portland. Its snowy peak rose above the gray clouds, and the setting sun caused its slopes to glisten with gold.

Salem was a small city of twenty thousand people with provincial attitudes and values. I'd never seen so many churches for such a little town. Despite being 1964, we ran into numerous refusals before someone would rent a place to an unmarried couple! In an absurd way, this led to our seriously considering marriage. The large one-way streets seemed odd, as if Salem wanted to be like Portland, but couldn't pull it off. Some people said that Salem lived in Portland's shadow, which seemed to ring true.

There were beautiful parks, precisely trimmed lawns and shrubbery. It was quiet and peaceful as we walked around searching for a hotel. In an attempt to control pedestrians' behavior, wait-on-curb signs were stenciled on the opposite side of the streets on every corner.

After a good night's sleep at the Senator Hotel, we contacted a real estate agent, and he facilitated our renting a furnished apartment at 1109 Oak Street for a hundred fifty dollars per month.

It had a kitchen, bath, living room, bedroom, and porch. Good old Mr Sanford was our neighbor. He was a friendly retired widower. He asked me, "Where's the Mrs?" I said, "We're not married," expecting him to shun me. To my surprise, he said, "Not married, I don't care. That's your business." He then shared his view of Salemites. "The people are odd here. I think they've been marrying cousins for the past century. They are judgmental and suffer from guilt! They want to be perfect, and they work on their lawns and houses all the time in order to have the best. They paint their houses every other month and focus on having the most immaculate flower gardens. If you don't have a smug face and two thousand roses in your yard, you are not a true Salemite! They'll ask you which church you go to before learning your name. And you had better go to a church because everyone does. You better not drink or at least be seen drinking. And you know you can't live together and have sex if you are not married." It turned out to be a joy to share meals and drinks with our atypical new friend Mr Sanford.

I called Dr Hoffstetter, the clinical psychologist to whom I was assigned at the correctional institution. On the phone, he seemed warm and sensitive. I shared my worries with him about having no money, no work for Lynn, and the difficulties finding a place to live with her. Mr Hoffstetter was understanding and said that I ought not to worry: everything would be all right. He even came over to visit and listen. "Here's twenty dollars." he said, "Having six kids, that's all I can spare at the moment, but if you need anything just call." Wow! The person I was going to work for was like Mr Sanford: kind, honest, accepting, and not hypocritical. Later that evening, Mr Sanford gave Lynn a long-stemmed yellow rose and said, "Everything will be fine!"

However, Lynn and I had problems in our intimate relationship. Although beautiful, she thought she was ugly and fat. My latent inner psychiatrist attempted to help, but I was, unknowingly, in over my head. Lynn also couldn't find work, as she wouldn't accept jobs offered to her, like being a waitress. So she suffered and acted the part of a frustrated wife. Today, she would be called a desperate housewife.

My work at the prison was exciting, frightening and challenging. I had to overcome my fear of possibly killing another man, as I went through the basic training for guards. I learned how to scramble and get armed in case of a riot. At the prison shooting range, I mastered loading and firing a hand gun, a twelve-gauge shot gun, tear gas, and even a machine gun. I passed a self-defense test, which meant I could theoretically fight off an attacker using karate. In contrast to my becoming more confident as a working man, Lynn was trying to be a traditional stay-at-home woman. It was an unexpected and ironic turn of events.

I was expected to write a research paper for my work-study course, which typically was qualitative or theoretical. However, I decided to carry out a scientific project, studying attempted suicide among the inmates. Dr Hoffstetter was supportive and facilitated my giving and scoring the MMPI psychological test to all the inmates involved in the study. It was an ambitious and rewarding project, which ended up as a paper entitled, "The Endeavor to Murder the Self: Research on Attempted Suicide at the Oregon Correctional Institution."[2] Through the University of Washington, I received an A for my work. Although the paper was never published, it was helpful to Dr Hoffstetter in understanding the problem and preventing further suicide attempts. For me personally, it continued my study of the phenomenon of suicide. This would culminate in a career in academia focused, in part, on how to best help suicidally-depressed individuals to overcome a wish to kill themselves.

The research involved structured interviews. I used the opportunity to help the inmates gain insight and understanding into their problems, with the hope of preventing future suicide attempts. This study crystallized my desire to become a psychiatrist or a clinical psychologist. I particularly liked treating the inmates as unique human beings. I enjoyed finding out what creative talents they had and encouraged their expression. For example, one inmate wrote poetry and gave me this poem:

The rose, the rose,
How grand it grows.
Despite the thorns,
The beauty of the flower.

In discussing his poem the inmate said, "Everybody has to grow up and accept their faults, yet be all they can be."

Walls
all around —
a rose blooms

I was very moved, while working in the prison, to realize that there was little difference between those in and out of prison. At least that was the case at the Oregon Correctional Institution. The inmates were men between the ages of eighteen and thirty, all sentenced to less than ten years. Three types of criminals were not accepted: those who had committed first degree murder, rape by force or treason. It was an institution that focused on treatment and rehabilitation. As a result of this experience, I would take courses in abnormal psychology and criminology at the University of California in Berkeley.

At the end of the summer, we left Salem for the final WICHE meeting in Seattle at the University of Washington. Afterwards, we headed south to Berkeley, California, which would be our home for the next two years.

Real or not —
love
persists

NOTES

1 Allen Wheelis, *How People Change* (New York: Harper & Row, 1973).

2 This paper is in my archives at the Cushing Memorial Library at Texas A & M University in College Station, Texas.

18

UC Berkeley and Free Speech

A serious daring starts from within.

EUDORA WELTY
One Writer's Beginnings

Sometimes after you arrive somewhere, you think, "Why didn't I just come here in the first place?" That's exactly how I felt about the University of California (UC), Berkeley. It felt like a home I was returning to, and its mascot, a bear, fit me well. I was going to hunker down, hibernate and study my pre-med and psychology classes so well that I'd get into medical school or graduate school in clinical psychology. UC made both of us happy. The UC campus was beautiful. The university and city were open to new ideas, the arts and cultures from around the world. Lynn had planned to go to graduate school in Drama at UC, but she missed the application deadline. Instead, she shifted to the more fun and practical path of being involved in the early days of the American Conservatory Theater (ACT) in San Francisco.

When I registered for my classes I was assigned a pre-med advisor, John Lawrence, MD, who was Head of Medical Physics. I know this was synchronicity because Dr Lawrence had a huge impact on my education at UC and on my entire life. He was a kind, gentle and wise soul, as well as a father surrogate. Soon after we met he said, "You're a junior and you have to pick a major." I said, "I don't know what to choose, as I like so many subjects." I explained that I was seriously interested in international relations, psychology, biology, and other pre-med courses. I was taking zoology, chemistry, physics, and German, but I also wanted to take abnormal psychology, criminology, and classes in literature and international politics.

After many frustrating hours of working with me to figure out what I'd major in, out of desperation, Dr Lawrence came up with an innovative solution. He said, "Several years ago I advised another student who wasn't able to restrict his interests to one subject, and he created his own Individual Major." I asked, "What's that?" Dr Lawrence showed me the section on Individual Majors in the undergraduate catalog. I liked what I read. I had to create a major and a four-year curriculum, along with an essay justifying it. Thus I developed an Individual Major in Psychological-Biological Sciences. I incorporated all my classes at

Shimer College, the University of Copenhagen, Whittier College, and the University of Washington, with the pre-med and psychology pre-requisites for medical school or graduate school in clinical psychology. I also integrated other subjects that I wanted to take. After I completed the outline of the curriculum and my essay to Dr Lawrence's satisfaction, he took it all over to the Dean of the College of Letters and Sciences for approval. To my amazement, my major was endorsed!

As a result of this development and the supportive mentoring by Dr Lawrence, I worked hard and excelled in my classes. My studies and a political uprising kept me busy, and Lynn's theater activities occupied much of her time.

In German Literature, we read *The Sorrows of Young Werther* in Johann Wolfgang von Goethe's original tongue. This book and its author influenced me greatly. Knowing German allowed me to travel and conduct research later on. Being a quarter German drew me to immerse myself in the language and culture. I'm sure this was a factor in my attraction to Carl Jung and desire to become an analytical psychologist. Perhaps it was destiny too, as I would become the first endowed professor of analytical psychology in the world.[1]

A small revolution called the Free Speech Movement (FSM) occurred during the fall semester of 1964. The FSM arose out of an attempt by the UC Administration to restrict certain controversial student organizations from openly advocating their views on atheism or communism in Sproul Plaza, which was like the Hyde Park of Berkeley. When a leader of a student group was arrested, students spontaneously surrounded the campus police car. The campus police were unable to move, and the FSM was born.

I remember Mario Savio, a FSM leader and philosophy student who spoke eloquently and passionately from atop the dented-in police car. After weeks of protest, I recall Savio calling for a strike and sit-in that occurred in Sproul Hall. UC was closed down by the FSM, and classes were canceled for a short time. Often I was torn because I supported the FSM, yet I wanted to go to class to learn. I participated in the sit-in and remember Joan Baez singing "We Shall Overcome" in Sproul Hall. I felt fortunate to be there because it was an important time in American history. It revealed how vital students are to protecting our basic rights, like freedom of speech. Later, the same UC students protested and helped end the unjust war in Vietnam. Participating in direct political action while keeping up with my studies was a challenging, but essential and invigorating, lesson from my time at UC.

A calling
daring to be —
gentle grace

LYNN

Frequently Lynn and I discussed marriage, as she said that she wanted to be a wife and eventually a mother. This all sounded wonderful, and led to our marriage on October 31, 1964. Both Lynn and I came from broken homes and, in retrospect, it was magical thinking to assume that, by establishing a make-believe happy marriage, all would be well. So on Halloween, with a leap of faith and a lot of foolishness, we took the plunge and nearly drowned. On reflection, it was a giant trick-or-treat! We kept our masks on. I was only nineteen when I married Lynn, who was twenty-one. Arthur Miller's words apply equally well to me: "The lure of another identity and of losing oneself. … There was something mistaken in my life … I had married too young."[2]

Meaningfully and symbolically, both my parents, who had remarried each other five months earlier, attended our small wedding at the Unitarian Church in Kensington, near Berkeley. After the wedding and over the holidays, Lynn and I headed south to San Blas, Mexico, for our honeymoon. We were deeply in love, but it was not to last. However, existentially, does that matter? "Moments, moments, that is life" is a reasonable philosophy; our love was for moments, and real!

The New Year of 1965 ushered in another full semester of arduous coursework, my twentieth birthday and our first year of marriage.

Love —
mist and falling water …
"I do"

NOTES

1 Frank McMillan, *Finding Jung: Frank N. McMillan, Jr., A Life in Quest of the Lion* (College Station: Texas A&M University Press, 2012).

2 Arthur Miller, *Timebends: A Life* (London: Minerva, 1990), 294.

19

What Kind of Doctor to Be: MD or PhD?

One's mind, once stretched by a new idea, never regains its original dimensions.

EUDORA WELTY
One Writer's Beginnings

Over the summer of 1965, I took Organic Chemistry, which in spite of its notorious difficulty, I ended up liking so much that I took an advanced organic chemistry class in the fall semester.My last year at UC Berkeley was excellent. However, despite the joy of learning, I was filled with doubt and fear. Would I do well enough on the MCAT, (Medical College Admission Test) to get into medical school?

This story will humanize the MCAT ordeal. When the test was handed out in the huge auditorium, I looked at the first question and didn't know the answer. I thought that I would piss in my pants, so I turned in my test to one proctor and ran out and down the hall. I went into the first bathroom that I came to. I relieved myself, but only when I left did I realize that it was a women's bathroom. After I got "pissed off," I completed the MCAT and did well enough to get into medical school.

I still wasn't convinced that medicine (psychiatry) was the right career path for me. I wondered if I wouldn't be happier as a clinical psychologist. My physician advisor and my father both encouraged me to choose medicine. I ended up applying to ten medical schools and five PhD programs in clinical psychology. I got rejected by nine medical schools, but was accepted at the University of Missouri in Columbia. I was wait-listed at the University of California in San Francisco (UCSF). I was also accepted to one PhD program in clinical psychology, at the University of Georgia. I quickly accepted the position at the University of Missouri School of Medicine in Columbia, which didn't require Quantitative Analysis (UCSF did). This enabled me to drop the course and spend more time on my senior honor's research project in psychology.

In addition to my regular studies during 1965-1966, I wrote and submitted an essay entitled "The People's Republic of China's Representation in the United Nations" for the Owen D. Young Prize in International Relations. I won first place, and this manuscript was placed in the UC Berkeley Library Archives. This paper proposed that China be admitted to the United Nations.

Healer, searcher
researcher —
seeds sown

Looking back on my life at the time, overall it was good, though I smoked cigarettes, which I didn't like. What's more, I thought my marriage was okay, but there were problems. For instance, one day Lynn came home from San Francisco after visiting Gumps, an up-scale department store. She told me that she went up a stairway, turned a corner and saw a very beautiful woman. She stopped and looked at the woman, but then she realized it was a mirror! Looking back, this was sad and symbolic, but at the time I simply found it odd and filed it away.

We also didn't spend a lot of time together. Lynn was busy with the ACT in San Francisco, and I was overworked with my classes and extra-curricular activities, such as the Big Brother Program. I helped a fatherless thirteen-year-old boy named Robbie, who had been in trouble with the police. I met him three times a week after school and once on the weekends. I'd assist him with his homework and then play basketball or pool with him. We also went to parks and the beach just to have fun. The relationship worked, in part, because I had been down that same path.

During my last year at UC, I read two important books. The first was Carl Jung's autobiography *Memories, Dreams, Reflections* and the second was the *Tao Te Ching* by Lao Tzu. I made extensive notes about how these two volumes were similar. Carl Jung and his psychology seemed Taoist. This seed grew and developed into a research project that ultimately evolved into a book, *The Tao of Jung*.[1]

Graduation was memorable. My Individual Major in Psychological-Biological Sciences was acknowledged as a one-of-a-kind degree, and the statesman Adlai Stevenson gave the commencement address. I was up close, so I could see before he spoke that he had a hole in the sole of one of his shoes. But still, it pained me that my parents were not in attendance.

During the summer of 1966, after my

graduation and prior to starting medical school, Lynn and I planned an extended European vacation, which both of us needed.

Pausing
in sun—
buds about to open

NOTES

1 David H. Rosen, *The Tao of Jung: The Way of Integrity* (New York: Arkana/Penguin, 1997).

20

Returning to Europe with my First Wife

All true things must change
and only that which changes remains true.

CARL JUNG
The Collected Works of C. G. Jung
Volume 14

Lynn and I packed our things into a rented U-haul trailer, and, following tearful goodbyes to friends, we headed for Springfield, Missouri. We stored everything at my parents' home. After a nice but brief visit, we drove east to Lynn's hometown of Lenox, Massachusetts, where we visited her family.

While it was not easy for me to leave Berkeley, I looked forward to the challenge of becoming a physician. It was more difficult for Lynn to move away from the Bay Area where she was involved in ACT and had made meaningful connections in the theater world. Lynn felt that nothing awaited her in Columbia, Missouri, and feared that it would be a repeat of our disappointing experience in Salem. I attempted to reassure her by pointing out that the University of Missouri had a theater arts department where she could pursue her former goal of attending graduate school. But that was my idea, not hers.

I had worked extremely hard on my studies for two years, so during the summer of 1966 I wanted to travel and have fun before starting medical school. We decided to go to Europe, and Lynn seemed excited, as she had never been there. I wanted Lynn to meet my Danish and Greek families and the family I'd met in East Berlin while traveling from Copenhagen. I'd been corresponding with the Spiess', and they wanted us to go with them on their vacation in East Germany.

On July 1, we flew to Copenhagen and spent a lovely week visiting my old host family. While in Copenhagen, we went to the German Democratic Republic (GDR) Embassy to get visas for our two-week vacation. At first the puzzled East Germans wondered why we Americans wanted to spend a holiday in their country, especially with a family. However, once they learned that I was from UC Berkeley and supported the Free Speech Movement, and had traveled to East Berlin and the Soviet Union two years earlier, they prepared our visas, calling us "student radicals!"

After saying goodbye and hugging my Danish family, we flew from Copenhagen to East Berlin on a Czechoslovakian airline, which had excellent service. Ruth met us at ten that night and checked us in at the Hotel Berolina, costing us the equivalent of $8.30 for the night (thirty-five East-German marks at 4.2 marks to the dollar). She then took us to their apartment on Karl Marx Allee. We gave the family gifts and said goodnight to twelve-year-old Cornelia and seven-year-old Rainer, who went to bed. The four of us stayed up all night drinking, eating, talking, and laughing. At five o'clock in the morning, Siegfried drove us to our hotel!

We slept late the next day and again returned to the Spiess' for more fun and to plan our vacation. First, we would head south to Weimar, then Leipzig, back to East Berlin, and then north to the Baltic Sea. On July 24, Lynn and I would leave Dresden by train to Prague.

We toured East Berlin for two days and saw the Karl Marx Platz near the Brandenburg Gate, the *Dom* (cathedral), and the Pergamon Museum. Ruth and Siegfried took their two children to their maternal grandparents, as their car was too small for six. This also allowed them to spend time with just us. We departed for Weimar, the birthplace of Goethe and Schiller and the home of the National Theater, something Lynn wanted to see. Weimar was a beautiful city of sixty thousand. We had supper and beer in the Black Bear Inn and saw the Gooseman Fountain across from Schiller's house. As I was fond of Goethe's work, I was thrilled to see his birthplace and *Rosengarten*.

Although it was difficult and sad, we visited Buchenwald, a Nazi concentration camp where two hundred fifty thousand inmates passed under the entrance gate that said, "*Jedem das Seine*" (literally, "to each his own," but figuratively, "everyone gets what they deserve"). Many thousands of them were killed, and I found it hard to believe what had happened in this ungodly place. To prevent it from happening again, everyone ought to see this horror. Going to the opposite, we then went to Wartburg, the most beautiful castle in all of Germany.

We headed back to Weimar at dusk for dinner at another old inn, where we had a great time eating and drinking beer. One old man said, "These GDR cigarettes are the best in the world; only the paper and the tobacco are bad!"

We then returned to East Berlin and stayed overnight at the Spiess's place. Lynn and I slept in the children's beds, and I was very touched by Ruth's goodnight greeting, "Your dreams will come true because this is the first time that you have slept under our roof."

The next morning, we headed north to the Baltic Sea and spent the night in Stralsund at the Baltic Hotel. We went to a beach where I swam with Siegfried, while Ruth and Lynn lay out in the sun. Ruth validated my career choice by saying, "I'm stronger psychologically since I met you and through our correspondence. It was like I was in a prison, and after meeting you, the burden was easier to bear. You helped me so much." She continued to feel positive about us and my relationship with Lynn. Ruth had just written her parents a postcard saying, "It is so beautiful — beyond description. These are days of merriment and reflection."

The next couple of days we spent in Hiddensee, an island off Rügen near Stralsund. The Communists allowed for an isle of beauty and freedom, with no cars or distractions from nature. It reminded me of the savage land in *Brave New World*. Hiddensee was one of the loveliest islands that I have ever visited. It was like Big Sur, but an island with golden sandy beaches. Cypress trees dipped into the sea, and the hazy blue sky was striking against the deep green of the cliffs. The atmosphere was raw and refreshing, and people were free and happy. There was even a nude public beach on the far side of the island!

On our way back to Berlin, we discussed religion. Siegfried said he didn't believe in God. Ruth was an agnostic. I explained that "My God is not a person, but rather a hope and positive belief in the good of humanity: a creative spirit and energy. Spiritual energy is never lost. An old person dies and a young tree grows." I could tell that Ruth liked my spiritual philosophy, and Siegfried clearly understood and respected my views.

On Sunday July 24, we went to Dresden and ate at Luisenhof, the best restaurant in East Germany. It sits on top of a mountain overlooking the city and the Elbe River. Afterwards,

Siegfried bought a massive amount of food for us to take on the train to Prague. We hugged and said goodbye. Ruth and Lynn shed tears while Siegfried and I held ours back, but we were crying inside. Once we got inside the train, I couldn't help exclaiming to Lynn, "Ruth and Siegfried are such strong, warm and wonderful individuals."

The train ride down the Elbe River to Prague was rich in natural beauty, with high cliffs on one side and sloping hills on the other. There were vineyards, castles and the setting sun. Five hours later, we arrived in Prague at midnight. We stayed at the Druzba Hotel for only $2.40 a night.

The next day we spent walking around the elegant city of spires. Prague is truly a treasure of art and architecture. We departed to Hungary in the morning by train, but had to stand up for four hours during the ride to Budapest, where we stayed at a student hotel for a dollar. I was exhausted, and Lynn felt sick to her stomach and cried. I think the poverty, repression and armed soldiers everywhere got to both of us.

The next day, we moved to a beautiful old room in a family's home for three dollars a night. We walked to a castle and a Catholic church, where services were being held. The following day, we caught a train to Beograd (Belgrade). Yugoslavia, known as "Little America," was full of spice, flavor and initiative. The people liked their leader, Tito, and the economy was better. There were open markets with plenty of everything! You could buy *The New York Times* and *Pravda*! We had dinner of lamb roast, vegetables, rice soup, salad, bread and butter, and a bottle of red wine for $3.40; a room at a student hotel cost $3.60.

Before we left for Thessaloniki, Greece, the next morning, we saw a diesel locomotive, a rare site in Eastern Europe, with an emblem of two hands shaking and a sign in English and Serbian, "Given by USA for friendship between Yugoslavia and USA." It seemed like a perfect reflection of the hope we were both feeling. On our way to to Greece, the Bulgarian countryside was scenic, sort of what I imagined Northern Italy and Switzerland to be like, with high mountains, streams and green fields. After we arrived, we checked in at Hotel Rex, and the next morning we went to Agia Triada by boat. For three days we rested, swam, sun-tanned on the beach, and began to recuperate. We loved the green trees, blue sky, special light, and raspberry blue sea. Lynn and I both felt better in this ancient birthplace of democracy. Free at last! We recovered and slowly made love.

We relished our days at Agia Triada, soaking up the healing Greek sun. Our nights were spent walking around Thessaloniki. The waterfront is refreshing, with the ocean right in front of us and no railing on the sea wall. The white tower and old arch, connected to a wall built two thousand years ago to surround the city, still stand. We ate at typical *tavernes*, which served classic and tasty Greek meals of *moussaka*, stuffed peppers, tomato and cucumber salad, bread, and melon. No longer depressed, it was symptomatic that I had my beard shaved and bought Lynn a necklace of shells.

The second night, we rested in our room at the Hotel Rex. Lynn exclaimed, "It's like heaven!" She was crying, she was so happy, and I felt closer to her. In two words: Greece heals!

I awoke late in the night and went out alone, which is my time for communion and being one with all. I walked up a hill on a cobblestone street to the source of some Greek music, which I'd heard below. I walked into the *taverna* named Café Greco, and an elderly man asked if I was from Germany. "O*hi* (no)," I answered. Then he and another old friend started guessing where I came from: France, (*ohi*), England, (*ohi*), Italy, (*ohi*), and Greece, (*ohi*). Finally Casanova, a young boy, said, "America!" "*Malista* (yes)," I replied. The waiter who looked a bit like a walrus asked, "What's your name?" "David," I replied. He said, "You're from Israel, not America." I said, "No, many Americans are named David." But he said, "They are also from Israel." Then in an attempt to clarify things, Casanova asked, "Where was your father born?" All I had time to say was, "Romania," before walrus-man said, "That's it, Israel to Romania and on to America. You are Israeli!" I replied, "Adam and Eve were from Israel, so we are all Israeli!" He and everyone laughed. There was an historical context for the Israeli comment; the Jews in Thessaloniki were rounded up and killed by the Nazis. On the way back to the Hotel Rex, I saw a strange sight at a sidewalk café: a man was sitting outside with a bear on a leash!

We left Thessaloniki by train for Athens. A crippled man sitting across from us said that he wept when Kennedy was murdered. He bought us drinks on the way. In Athens, I called Alex at the Notara Street apartment. After many rings, he answered, breathless. He said, "I waited for you this morning. Now I'm loving this Swedish girl, so I'll come and get you in thirty minutes." Smiling to myself as I recalled similar circumstances in the past, I said, "Sorry to interrupt and that's fine."

Alex arrived one and a half hours later, which is "on time" in Greece! My dear Greek brother was with his Swedish girlfriend, and we had drinks at a sidewalk café. Then we all headed to Alex's new family home in Kifissia, which was spacious and built with marble from Pentali, the same marble used to build the Parthenon. The view of Athens was spectacular! For our noon meal, my Greek mother made her delicious chicken à la Greco. It was so nice to renew my connection with my Greek family and have them meet Lynn. After a nap we went to central Athens and visited the Acropolis by full moonlight. It felt like the gods were with us. It was an awesome experience. Lynn was so overcome with joy that tears ran down her cheeks. Under the full moon, we spent nearly two hours amongst the ruins.

We spent two more days in Athens and visited the phenomenal National Archeological Museum, the Market and the outdoor theater at the Acropolis, where we saw a moving production of *Oedipus Rex*. We also walked up a central hill, Lycabettus, for a panoramic view of Athens at night with its unique light. That night Lynn and I renewed our marital vows. On our last day, we went to Rafina, a nearby beach, to swim and continue to feel the healing rays of the sun.

The sun sets—
yes
she is the one

Alex helped us buy food and drinks on the evening of August 4, when we left by boat for Crete. We staked out our own bench in deck class. Greeks were dancing with live bouzouki music. It was a joyous ride to Crete on a calm Aegean Sea. Lynn and I ate, drank, laughed, talked, and slept head-to-feet. At nine o'clock the next morning, we arrived in Crete at the port city of Iraklion. It was hot, but we walked around the city, got a room at Pension Minos, and rented a motor scooter for a week. Crete was magical!

The first place we visited was Knossos, an ancient and vast palace on a hill built by the Minoans in 2000 to 1600 BCE. It was a matriarchal culture. The people were very short, and I had to duck my head to get through doorways. The Minoans had a bustling and advanced civilization. Their artful frescoes revealed a warless society with a focus on beauty and the arts. Their jewelry, ceramics and sculpture work was advanced, as was their theater: what appeared to be religious plays. The Minoans had tweezers, safety pins, needles, utensils, and tools. They also had inside toilets, bathtubs and a sewer system. Common symbols of the Minoans were the sacred bull, the two-headed axe and a six-pointed star like the Star of David.

Next we went to Malia, one of the finest beaches in Greece. Then on the way to Neapolis, we picked some ripe figs. We stayed on a rooftop in Ierapetra for the night at a cost of fifteen drachmas, or about fifty cents. We had the sky for a blanket, with a yellow moon, the Big Dipper and the Milky Way. Love and a warm breeze made for a delightful and refreshing sleep.

Lynn and I woke up to nearby church bells and a rising sun. We drove our scooter east of Ierapetra to the southern shoreline of Crete and went to a beach near the Bishop's mansion. The sea was emerald blue, and the beach had little smooth pebbles of all colors.

It was a burning hot 110 degrees on the way to Ierapetra, and very little grew in the harsh surroundings. We returned to a cooler and greener Malia for the night. After a delicious meal of *moussaka*, stuffed tomatoes, salad, and a bottle of Minos wine, we headed to the beach and swam with the stars above us.

The next day, we swam a lot in the warm crystal clear sea. We even ventured out to the island of the Church of Transfiguration. Lynn lay in the sun, and I sketched. We again slept on a roof top and woke up at sunrise. My eyes opened from a night dream to another dream:

CHURCH ISLAND, MALIA, CRETE

an orange ball of fire rising slowly in the Aegean sky. It was a blending of yellow, orange, red, and many shades of blue. It felt like we were in a romantic movie.

The next day we drove to Rethymnon, which was strikingly different from other Greek towns. The architecture was medieval and Turkish with minarets and very narrow streets. I was in a bad mood, and we sat on the wall by the sea. Lynn was very understanding about my fears and self-doubts regarding medical school. She was reassuring and supportive. She said, "You got into medical school! All experiences are good; take from it what is valuable." I was aware that my fears regarding medical school involved a conflict with my father. Lynn said, "It will work itself out, and probably he has more respect for you now!" This was true, but I had not worked out my conflict with authority.

The last night in Crete was beset by the thought, "I hate to leave this place. I feel quite comfortable here." Our final day in Crete was spent in Kastelli. We stopped on the way for bunches of purple grapes, which Lynn fed to me as we sped along the ocean and winding mountain roads. I thought about my wife and goals of having a nice home and children. I also thought about becoming a psychiatrist and being able to talk with people who needed help. I did not yet realize that most people who want to be psychiatrists and psychologists are emotionally disturbed themselves.

The boat back from Crete to Piraeus, the port of Athens, was again smooth. It was warm on the deck where we slept. We took the bus to Kifissia. It was good to be with Alex and his family again. The next day, Alex took us to see *The Trojan Women* by Euripides in the ancient theater at the Acropolis. It was superb, and Lynn cried because she was so moved.

For the following five days, I took Lynn on an adventure to some of Greece's best archeological sites. First we went by bus to Delphi, which is magnificent. Then we went by Greek railway to Olympia, which was "quiet, moist and raw," as noted in my journal. We went on to Andritsena via Pyrgos and hitch-hiked a ride to Bassae with a French couple who were also traveling there. Bassae is the most beautiful and intact ancient building standing in all of Greece. A little-known and rarely visited temple, it is high up in the mountains close to the gods. We arrived at sunset, and it was majestic.

The French couple had the only vacant room in the nearby town, so that night they let us sleep in their car. In the morning, we washed in the water fountain of Andritsena. After Greek yogurt with honey, bread and coffee, we took buses to Nafplio via Tripoli.

From Nafplio, we hitched a ride to Epidaurus. Lynn loved the theater where fourteen thousand people can watch a play, and everyone can hear a whisper from the center stage to the top seat! After touring the healing temples and dream chambers of Epidaurus, we headed to Mycenae. I liked seeing the Lion's Gate again, as well as Agamemnon's tomb.

We caught the last bus back to Athens and stayed at Alex's Notara Street apartment. It was good to shower and rest. The next day, our last in Greece, was spent in Kifissia with Alex and his family.

On August 20, we were off to Brindisi, Italy, by boat again via deck class, to save money. It was cold and windy. A Greek boy felt sorry for us and took us to an inside area where he had extra blankets. I was too tired to care that I slept next to a murderer, one of four prisoners with three police, who was being taken to Corfu to serve two more years in prison. He had already served fifteen years in another prison. Though he killed someone when he was twenty-one, he received a short sentence because his family was wealthy.

From Brindisi, we took a train to Rome and stayed five days in a pensione. We walked the city: Saint Peter's Cathedral, the Vatican, Spanish Steps, Pantheon, Coliseum, Roman Forum, and many fountains (especially the Trevi Fountain). We ate an excellent four-course meal at Onarmos Restaurant for four hundred fifty lire, or seventy cents. We also went to an outdoor concert at the Basilica of Maxentius and Constantine. We enjoyed the music in this beautiful place. The National Academy of Saint

Cecilia performed Berlioz's *Roman Carnival*, Debussy's *Prelude to the Afternoon of a Faun*, Stravinsky's *The Fire Bird*, and Tchaikovsky's Sixth Symphony, *Pathétique*. It was awesome music and the seats were only five hundred lire, or eighty cents.

We spent one full day in the Vatican Museum, where we saw the Sistine Chapel and letters signed by Raphael and Galileo. We also visited the Catacombs of Saint Sebastian, which were built in the second and third centuries.

Our next stop was Florence. Florence easily became our favorite city in Italy, as we immersed ourselves in its ancient culture and art history. We loved seeing Michelangelo's *David* at The Academy of Fine Arts of Florence and his paintings at the Uffizi and Pitti Palace, as well as those of Leonardo da Vinci and many others.

From Florence, we traveled to Antwerp via a stopover in Köln (Cologne, West Germany). I loved being able to speak German again. We visited Marÿke and family in Antwerp and the next day went to Brussels for our flight to New York, as we made our way back to Missouri. In just two weeks I would begin my studies to become a medical doctor.

Am I a healer,
to others,
to myself?

21

First Year Medical Student

Medical school robbed me
of the best years of my life.

attributed to
CHE GUEVARA

After short visits with both our families, we got another U-haul and moved our things from Springfield to Columbia, Missouri. We gave ourselves two weeks, before I had to start medical school, to move into our new abode and get settled. We found a quonset hut, such a ubiquitous symbol of the times, which looked like a giant turtle from the outside. Inside we made it as attractive as possible, but you can only do so much with a tunnel shaped hut of corrugated steel and a cement floor. Rather primitive, it was symbolic of a prison where I had to do time: four years to be exact.

Living in a hollow home
emptiness
all around

At the orientation for the University of Missouri School of Medicine, I was struck by one of the slides in a presentation by an associate dean. It showed many kinds of people coming into the medical school, but going out they all looked the same! This was the era when doctors had lots of power and were ninety-five percent male. There were only two blacks in the four-year medical school: one was a male senior and the other a woman who was a freshman like me. She was a double minority. Tragically, the black woman, who won a national student research award, was dropped from the medical school after two years. To me, this seemed to be due to racial discrimination and sexism. Thankfully, so much has changed, and today nearly fifty percent of medical students are women. However, while blacks are better represented, their numbers are not even close to the proportion of blacks in society.

On the first day of gross anatomy, which was the primary course during the first semester, we were assigned a cadaver. Upon seeing a dead person, one student walked out, never to return. Confronting the cadaver demands that one establish a relationship with a deceased human being. It actually is the first doctor-patient relationship. Each one of us had to find a way, that is, a reason and a purpose, to cut on this dead person. I viewed the cadaver as a holy gift of learning. To me the human body dead or alive is sacred. I had created a bond with Leonardo da Vinci who, in fear of his own death, dissected bodies and drew what he saw. I occasionally returned to the anatomy room alone at night and drew what I dissected. It helped me learn. I couldn't do this very often because I found out Lynn wasn't comfortable being alone. Since she wasn't in school or working, she was in need of me. I was torn. I wanted to study, but she wanted me with her. I really tried, but nothing I did was good enough.

Dissecting and
drawing—
sacred cadaver

In spite of my night-time efforts, I failed the first anatomy exam. The Chairman of Anatomy called me in and said, "I don't know what you did as an undergraduate, but you have to study in medical school." So I shifted from fifty percent studying and fifty percent being with Lynn to ninety percent studying and ten percent time with Lynn. This change caused Lynn to become very upset and depressed.

FIRST YEAR OF MEDICAL SCHOOL

One night I was supposed to get home at seven-thirty for dinner, and it was eight-thirty when I arrived. Lynn flipped out and threw the spaghetti she had made all over the kitchen end of the Quonset hut. She screamed, “If you want to eat, then you can scrape it off the wall and floor!”

The trouble at home made me study even harder, which did wonders for my performance in GrossAnatomy, and I ended up getting honors. My marriage, however, suffered greatly. The stress and strain only increased over the first year. I thought if we got a dog, it might help keep Lynn company. We got a cute little male mutt from the pound. We named him Zorba, but it helped only a little. I think the seeds of our separation were sown during that time. While I was struggling through the Spring Semester with neuroanatomy, histology, biochemistry, and physiology, Lynn was planning her escape.

I did well in my classes, but I refused to go to the dog labs in physiology. I couldn’t run experiments on and kill dogs to learn things I could master from a textbook. Since I failed all the dog labs, the Chairman of Physiology called me in and said that if I didn’t get an A or B on the final exam, I’d fail the course. Fortunately, I did what was required, but I feel it was due as much to prayer as mastering content.

Would not kill dogs
to learn—
Zorba dances

Meanwhile, Lynn arranged with her former Whittier College Theater professor, who had subsequently moved to the University of South Carolina, to act in a summer stock theater on Hilton Head Island. This took place over the only official vacation time that I had during medical school, and Lynn didn’t want me to go with her. That seemed unacceptable, since she was my wife. I wanted to be with her on this resort island known for its beauty and beaches.

I arranged to get a summer fellowship in psychiatry in order to turn my senior honor’s thesis into a monograph, which would end up becoming my first published book.[1] This honor's project, "Lesbianism: A Study of Female Homosexuality," involved a community sample drawn from the Daughters of Bilitis. I chose this topic after going to a lecture at Stiles Hall by Phyllis Lyon, a "normal" lesbian. She talked about the need for research on lesbians, as Freud claimed that homosexuality was a mental illness. She, however, maintained that little or no research had been done on a non-psychiatric population.

The fellowship allowed me to do the work anywhere, so I accompanied Lynn to Hilton Head. Little did I know that it was the beginning of the end!

Into black cloud
storm brewing —
about to be lost

NOTES

1 David H. Rosen, *Lesbianism: A Study of Female Homosexuality* (Springfield, IL: Charles Thomas Publisher, 1974).

22

Summer of Death and Rebirth

If I am not for myself, who is for me?
And if I am for myself (only),
what then am I?

HILLEL
The Sayings of the Jewish Fathers
(*Pirke Aboth*)

During that spring of 1967, I naively thought it only strange that Lynn didn't want me to accompany her to Hilton Head while she performed in a summer stock repertoire theater. Now I realize that she had foretold what would transpire. The following is my journal entry dated March 25, 1966: "Lynn said when she was on stage, she felt free and wonderful inside. She added that were she to act again, she would have to leave me. That I cannot understand — because it's also my goal to have that attitude of freedom. Why shouldn't both of us live together, each with that free spirit inside?" Unfortunately (or fortunately), I insisted on accompanying her.

The first two weeks went well. Lynn was a star again, and I adored and supported her. However, after three weeks at Hilton Head, Lynn told me, "I don't want to go back to Missouri because I can't do what I want to do." I said, "Sure you can. What do you want to do?" Lynn answered, "Be able to put my feet up on a table and have my black panties show. Be able to go out at 4 AM and talk to whoever I want to. Be able to act and be in the theater, and I can't do that in Columbia, Missouri." I said, "Not true, there are good people in the theater there." She said (and she was right), "You don't understand me. I'm thinking about not going back. So you'll have to give me up." Again, a prophetic statement!

Love too young
breaks,
burns

Then Lynn started doing things to provoke me to reject and leave her. She stayed out all night and was intimate with the leading man in *Light up the Sky*, the first of three plays she was cast in as the lead. Early one morning when I was sleeping alone, she woke me to tell me she was going skinny dipping with three guys. Then, in bars or night clubs after the plays were over, she started moving away from me when I attempted to put my arm around her or give her a kiss. One night I was so mad that I left and went to the beach. I sat down by the sea, the great accepter and comforter. Of this, I wrote in my journal, "I see you happy, Lynn, but it's at the expense of our happiness and you push me away. Now I'm alone, all alone by the sea. I want to talk and be with Lynn. I want to love her. She is driving me crazy. Please help me God. Why this? What have I done or not done? Why must I suffer so? I feel like a giant fool!"

Reactively, I had a brief and intense relationship with an artist called Honey Bear. She was part of a summer art school and my pain became bearable temporarily. After painting my portrait, she, too, left me high and dry for another man, a painter in her program. So I again returned to the sea alone.

Alone—
me
and the sea

During those painful days, I had a scary dream: I was in the military and was told to meet some interns. The interns threw their arms around me. I asked, "Who are the interns?" I was told, "The people who want to commit suicide."

Interns … yes, "turn inward." Now it seems so obvious. This dream connected me to my troubled father (military) and a murderous rage that was turning in on myself. It was a horrific dream foretelling what was about to happen.

The next night, I had the following dream, which turned out to be a gift from God. It concerned how I would eventually resolve the crisis with Lynn at Hilton Head. A beautiful mature glowing woman was sitting across from me staring into my eyes. She said, "Love, David, love as you are. Go free."

Subsequently, I found a note written by Lynn. "I'm not the same Lynn you married. I've changed so I can be on the stage. Also, I'm not having any children." This message saddened me greatly. Lynn had promised when we married to have our children. I felt betrayed and waves of despair washed over me.

Feeling deep loneliness … I woke up before dawn and wrote, "Prepare yourself for Hell, then you'll be ready for Heaven." Later that night, as I sat waiting for Lynn in a bar, she walked in with her leading man. Ignoring me, she went on to demonstrate that her romantic involvement with this man did not stop when the acting did. I watched the two of them, afraid of what might happen if I vented my rage. Then I ran out of the bar, jumped into my car and sped wildly through the narrow and winding island roads. I envisioned crashing into an embankment, or going off a bridge, thinking death would be far better than the pain I was experiencing.

Then something very unusual happened. I spun the car into a field, stopped it, got out, and began running through the moonlit, jungle-like terrain. As I ran, I could see myself from above, disappearing and reappearing beneath the trees. The quality of the vision, and with it my state of mind, became clearer and clearer, until finally I heard a voice say, "Leave!"

I later came to realize that this inner voice issued forth from my soul, the divine center of my psyche or Self according to Jung. That uncanny experience remains my only out-of-body experience. I now understand out-of-body to be beyond ego, ego being first a representation of body. Through this peak experience, I unwittingly found my anima (my soul, and the "love" woman of my dream), and my Self found me. My self-preservation instinct took command of my destiny.

I left Hilton Head within one hour, knowing and accepting that my marriage was in dire straits. But the fact that I survived did not mean that my heart was spared feelings of helplessness and worthlessness. I drove to New York City and consulted a psychiatrist, who was also a family friend. I found myself saying words to him that most severely depressed people say to themselves: "I'm a failure. It's hopeless. Why live?" His reply was simple and wise, and it has shaped my response to many setbacks ever since. "You are not a failure," he said. "You failed at marriage."

I wish I had been strong enough to sever my relationship with Lynn sooner rather than later. My rational mind and compassionate nature coupled with my feelings of insecurity and inadequacy. As a result, I told myself to give her another chance. In fact, I was frightened of being by myself. I begged her to come back and give up her stipend to attend graduate school in theater at the University of South Carolina, which was, ironically, in Columbia, South Carolina. I even got her mother June, and best friend Judy, to visit her there and convince her to return to her husband in Columbia, Missouri. It worked, but led to a year of hell on earth!

When I picked Lynn up at the bus station in Saint Louis on September 1, 1967, she told me of affairs with other men, and I wondered why I had asked her to come back. She then revealed that the reason she returned was because Jeff, the leading man she loved, didn't want her to live with him in the other Columbia. I asked, "That's why you came back — not because you love me?" "Yes," she cruelly disclosed.

So the long and painful process of sorting out my relationship with Lynn began, while I was involved in an extremely demanding and difficult second year of medical school.

The pull
of failed love —
the tree falls

23

Parting of the Ways: Becoming Myself

There is no coming to consciousness without pain.

CARL JUNG
Contributions to Analytical Psychology

As the second year of medical school started, Lynn and I were close for several days. I began to have hope that maybe our relationship could be salvaged. Then she stunned me when she disclosed that she felt like she had wasted the last three years. She cried, "I'm nothing. I have nothing to offer. I'm ugly and fat. How can you stand to touch me?" In her cry for help, I felt her agony. I then realized that I was in over my head, and I went to see Dr Weiss, Chairman of Psychiatry. He recommended that we see Dr Ajans, a psychiatrist, for marital counseling.

At about this same time, my poet friend Sam Thomas came over to our place with a bottle of wine. He wanted to talk about problems with his wife and the fact that he hadn't been able to get his poetry published. I had to study for pathology and microbiology, so I hurriedly ended the conversation. Sam went home and stabbed himself seven times in the stomach, cut his right hand, and nearly cut off his left hand. His wife found him in a pool of blood, and he was rushed to the hospital. An operation and multiple sutures saved his life. When Lynn and I visited him in the hospital, I asked why he tried to kill himself. He said, "I had to make something happen. I threw my life to chance." Sam was never the same; it was as if his soul was gone. Six months later he hanged himself. This tragedy taught me the hard way: always take time to listen. As a tribute to him, I arranged for a book of his poems to be published.[1]

Sun shining through
blossoming cherry tree —
petals fall slowly

Even though I sensed that Lynn didn't want to be with me, I thought we ought to see if marital therapy could help us. Temporarily things did get better. However, two weeks later, after we visited my family home in Springfield, Missouri, the progress seemed to fall away. Lynn again asserted that she hated herself. I was at a complete loss. Lynn thought negatively about everything, which is reflected in these two comments: "Why did you make me return?" and "Columbia,

Missouri, is the worst place on earth." Lynn refused to get a job, and I was forced to take out a loan because we were in debt.

Things went from bad to worse. When I had to shave my beard due to a policy at the medical school, Lynn made it worse by asking, "Who are you?" I hated to acquiesce and change for an institution, and Lynn wouldn't come near me or hug and kiss me, which hurt deeply. Yet, either I shaved, or I would be dropped from the school. Once Lynn lost it and screamed, "Get away. Don't come near me." So I left and went to the medical school library. When I returned, she blasted me for leaving her! It was a no-win situation.

My journal entries are telling: "Lynn screams a lot and I hate it. Part of me is dead already. Our lives lead in opposite directions. I used to think we had a common spirit — not now. We are not alike. On November 12, 1967, Lynn wrote a love letter to one of her former summer beaus. I said to her that I felt rejected." I then knew that Lynn was using me, and I finally admitted to myself that she really didn't love me. I felt very alone, but close to God.

The situation with Lynn became more ominous on December 7, 1967, when she said, "I'm so alone and crying all the time. I'm desperate, frightened and I think I'll commit suicide." Early in 1968, Lynn started losing weight and kept dieting, until there was no more fat to lose. She got down to ninety-five pounds! At that point I felt frustrated and sensed that there was no sure path. Although I wanted to accept, forget, forgive, and understand, I found it increasingly difficult. I actually was increasingly concerned that Lynn might starve herself to death. However, she refused to continue marital therapy or seek psychiatric care for herself.

On March 31, 1968, President Lyndon Baines Johnson made a speech saying that he would not seek or accept his party's nomination as a presidential candidate. He said the Lord spoke to him and said, "Lyndon, go back to the ranch and rest in peace." Prompted by growing anti-Vietnam War demonstrations, he realized that a house divided against itself would fall.

Nature always provides healing moments. In the spring of 1968, we visited the medical student Tom Seddon's family farm near Mineral Fork Creek. At the time, we were discussing a separation, and I was distant from Lynn. Nevertheless, the healing power of nature was working on me. Early in the morning, when the sun was rising, I ventured out. I walked to the creek and sketched daffodils and saw what I thought was an angel. My journal contains haiku-like lines, though I didn't write my first haiku until ten years later. On April 1, 1968 I wrote:

Over the hill / down the meadow / valley green / Smell cedar / feel sun / hear branch snap / Dogwood buds / feel bark / rocks touch soul/ Flowers blossom / feet ache / ever present spirit.

I was also healing my mind through the mental stimulation I found by reading non-medical books. I read *Creative Evolution* by Henri Bergson, the winner of the Nobel Prize for Literature in 1928. He saw reality as durational: time is not man's illusion within a framework of eternity but a duration, an enduring present. Bergson said, "Duration forms the past and present into one organic whole and exhibits itself above all in memory, where the past survives in the present."[2] He also said, "For a conscious being to exist is to change, to change is to mature, to mature is to go on creating oneself endlessly."[3] Bergson thought that the soul was immortal and that energy could never be blotted out. In addition he said, "Memory must be, in principle, a power absolutely independent of matter. If, then, spirit is a reality, it is here, in the phenomenon of memory, that we may come into touch with it experimentally."[4] A seed was planted, and twenty-three years later I would publish a scientific study supporting Bergson's theory.[5]

The reason I like Henri Bergson so much is that he is like Carl Jung, Johann Wolfgang von Goethe, William James, Abraham Maslow, and Viktor Frankl, all of whom were vital to my own development. Together they affirmed what I knew and would know! I loved Bergson's concept of the *élan vital* or *vital spark*, which is close to the meaning of soul and Jung's central archetype of the Self. Bergson said, "God is unceasing life, action and freedom. Creation, so conceived, is not a mystery; we experience it ourselves when we act freely."[6] This is a great description of the Creator and how spiritual meaning is linked to freedom.

It was quite revealing to read in my journal the list of writers who influenced me at a young age. Above all were Carl Jung, William Osler, William Carlos Williams, John Keats, Sigmund Freud, Karl Menninger, Frieda Fromm-Reichmann, Wendell Holmes, Anton Chekhov, William James, and Somerset Maughan. Also included in the list were J.D. Salinger, Ken Kesey, Henry Miller, Thomas Mann, Hermann Hesse, Martin Buber, Franz Kafka, Johann Wolfgang von Goethe, Anaïs Nin, William Shakespeare, Baruch Spinoza, William Butler Yeats, William Blake, James Joyce, Leo Tolstoy, Fyodor Dostoevsky, Michel de Montaigne, Rainer M. Rilke, D.H. Lawrence, Kenneth Patchen, Aldous Huxley, Erik Erikson, Allen Ginsberg, Lawrence Ferlinghetti, Walt Whitman, John Dewey, Lawrence Durrell, Dylan Thomas, T.S. Eliot, Ralph Waldo Emerson, Lao Tzu, Henry David Thoreau, and Teilhard de Chardin. These authors helped to balance the reductionist scientific curriculum of medical school.

On April 4, 1968, I heard on the news that Martin Luther King, Jr suffered the same fate as Gandhi, whose non-violent ways he followed. I was deeply saddened by the assassination of Dr King, who received the Nobel Peace Prize in 1964 and had a dream of a world without racial barriers. On April 7, I attended a memorial service for him. We sang "We Shall Overcome," and I sobbed uncontrollably, as I did when I first heard of his untimely and calamitous death in Memphis.

At that time, I was taking Physical Diagnosis in preparation for the clinical years of medical school. The first patient was a thirty-year-old extremely thin man with a dark complexion. We were told to palpate his huge spleen, the result of chronic myelogenous leukemia. As there was no cure, tragically he had only a short time to live. He looked like a concentration camp victim. We all felt his spleen, but I was the last. I lingered and touched my hands softly to his abdomen; I wanted him to know the compassion I felt toward him. Our eyes met, and I saw the fear of death in them. His eyes seemed to scream, "Help me." It was very sad to think that all I could do was connect with the small amount of hope I saw in his soulful blue eyes.

Later that month, on April 11, I won the election for junior class president by one vote! I felt that they voted for change: in spirit, in student responsibility and in medical education.

I was already the president of the radical Student Health Organization (SHO), which organized and staffed a free health clinic in Columbia, Missouri. Following President Kennedy's Medicare legislation, SHO maintained that health care was a right. Sadly this was a reality only for the elderly. Kennedy was shot before he could institute Medicare for everyone, so that we would have a health care system like Canada.

In the meantime, Lynn was destroying herself by not eating. Just before she left to visit her mother on June 27, she forecasted doom. She said, "I'm on a bridge and I'm in the center. If I go to either end it will collapse, and I'll fall into the deep gorge below. On one end is the dependency of marriage. On the other end is the independence of acting and self-destruction."

We talked about divorce, but she said that I would have to initiate it. On her return Lynn said, "I feel like I'm fading away. I'm hollow inside where my self used to be. I don't know who I am. Everything I am seems unreal: woman, wife, actress." I was concerned and bothered by Lynn's statements. She often said, "I need help," but refused to seek it.

She told me that her problem went back to age nineteen, when she was a sophomore in college and felt the very same way: "Like a zero, nothing, and that it would be better to commit suicide." I had not realized that Lynn's condition predated my knowing her. I felt betrayed again and hopeless. Of course, I had also betrayed myself by asking her to return after our infidelities during the summer at Hilton Head. I have since learned that without betrayal — including that greatest teacher of all: self-betrayal — we cannot experience trust. As Hillman maintains, "Wherever there is trust in a union, the risk of betrayal becomes a real possibility."[7] "The healing power of betrayal is a forgiving that is not a forgetting, but the remembrance of wrong transformed within a wider context, or as Jung has put it, 'the salt of bitterness transformed into the salt of wisdom.'"[8] Hillman continues, "Just as trust had within it the seed of betrayal, so betrayal has within it the seed of forgiveness."[9]

I have forgiven Lynn, and I hope she has been fulfilled in her life. The last I heard, she was married to an older man, had no children and kept the name "Lynn Rosen" for her work as a TV News reporter. It's noteworthy that, after I was betrayed, I entered psychotherapy in order to forgive Lynn. How could I live fully without renewed trust and hope? I agree with Hillman that betrayal, of other or self, cries out for forgiveness, "the highest of religious feelings."[10] Hillman adds the caveat, "But forgiveness is so difficult that it probably needs some help from the other person. I mean by this that the wrong, if not remembered by both parties — and remembered as a wrong — falls on the betrayed."[11]

During late June of that year, I had several dreams in which a tooth, or lots of teeth, fell out. Losing teeth symbolized the loss of old identities such as the too-dependent me, the nice guy and the husband at too young an age. The dreams also seemed to herald my becoming a "Jungian shaman," able to help myself and others recover one's true self.

At the beginning of July, I started the clinical years of medical school, which I loved. During each rotation — psychiatry, medicine, surgery, pediatrics and obstetrics, and gynecology — I felt more and more interested in each specialty. Becoming a physician was my calling, my vocation, instead of just a career. When I entered medical school, I wanted to be a psychiatrist. Little did I know then how distressed I was and how much help I needed. I am certain that this is why I became a Jungian psychoanalyst.

On October 3, I started an externship in psychiatry at the Menninger Clinic in Topeka, Kansas, in part to see if I wanted to do my residency in psychiatry there. Despite being a great program, I discovered it was too Freudian for me. However, I met and was taught by some of the greats in psychiatry and psychology: Otto Kernberg, Gardner Murphy, Paul Pryser, and Karl Menninger himself. Being away from Lynn turned out to be a godsend. It allowed time for me to grow and develop as my real self.

I began the process of divorcing Lynn. Synchronistically, on November 26, two days before I left Menninger's, Lynn told me that she had met a sculptor named Bill and ended up having an affair with him. In a real way this made the whole thing easier. I, too, had an affair with a harpist in Topeka named Anne. Ironically, Bill broke off the relationship at the same time I had the divorce papers served in early 1969. Lynn went into a suicidal tailspin! She left the house at night on March 15 and admitted herself to the psychiatric part of the hospital where I was, as a medical student, on a surgery rotation. As I cared about Lynn receiving the best treatment, within three days I facilitated a transfer to Menninger's, where she was helped immensely. Because I had been a student there and they were compassionate, I never received a bill for Lynn's treatment. For this I will be forever grateful.

On path
by myself
alone … all one

Two months later on May 8, while on obstetrics and gynecology, I delivered my first baby, a seven-and-a-half-pound healthy boy! Then, on May 24, my divorce from Lynn was decreed by the court. This signaled a death and rebirth experience for me. I applied for and accepted a research fellowship in suicidology at the University of Edinburgh, Scotland. I prepared to venture forth to New York, and on to Scotland and its healing isle of Iona. Before all else, Physician, heal thyself.[12]

NOTES

1 Sam Thomas, *Bits & Snatches: The Selected Work of Sam Thomas*, ed. Joel Weishaus (Brooklyn, NY: White Rose Press, 1974). This volume includes a postnote by Gary Snyder, who knew Sam and Joel.

2 Henri Bergson, *Creative Evolution*, trans. Arthur Mitchell (New York: Henry Holt & Company, 1911).

3 Ibid.

4 Ibid.

5 David H. Rosen, Steven M. Smith, Holly L. Huston, and Gilbert Gonzalez, "Empirical Study of Associations Between Symbols and Their Meanings: Evidence of Collective Unconscious (Archetypal) Memory," *Journal of Analytical Psychology* 36 (1991): 211-228.
Recently this study was replicated in Berne Switzerland by Milena Sotirova-Kohli et al. See "Symbol/Meaning Paired-Associate Recall: An 'Archetypal Memory' Advantage?" in online journal, *Behavioral Sciences*, 2013, 3, 541-561.

6 Henri Bergson, *Creative Evolution*, trans. Arthur Mitchell (New York: Henry Holt & Company, 1911).

7 James Hillman, "Betrayal," *SPRING: A Journal of Archetype and Culture* (1965): 52-76. First presented as Lecture 128 to The Guild for Pastoral Psychology in London on October, 1964, and published by the Guild.

8 Jung, quoted by Hillman, Ibid., 74.

9 Ibid.

10 Ibid., 73.

11 Ibid., 74.

12 Bible, *Luke 4:23* (King James Version).

24

Physician, Heal Thyself

The main reason for healing is love.

PARACELSUS
preface to
The Book of Hospitals

I loved to visit New York City and stay with my godparents, Sam and Claire Silverman. They did not have children of their own, and in times of imagining the simultaneous deaths of my parents, I relished the thought of being their only son. Sam, my father's best friend, was a Jew who had also grown up with immigrant parents on the Lower East Side. Sam's career had been stellar. He had become a New York Supreme Court Justice. This is an elected position, and once Bobby Kennedy campaigned for him. Claire was Catholic, and she became one of my mother's best friends. At Sam and Claire's, I always felt love and acceptance.

I also visited my artist friend Karil during my stay in New York City. She was the best friend of the artist I fell in love with during the summer after I was betrayed by Lynn. I was very fond of Karil, and she nurtured my identity as an artist. About this time, I dreamt that I was an artist and farmer. Now I realize that I am an artist; I have always drawn and painted. I also enjoy growing plants, especially flowers and trees. Knowing that I was going to Scotland, Karil wanted me to meet her great aunt, who was a widow and British noblewoman. She had been married to the American consul in Edinburgh, Scotland. We had high tea together and a meaningful conversation. I've never been good at hiding my emotions, so she felt my depression and learned of my recent divorce. Sensing that I was in need of healing, she leaned toward me, and with her lovely English accent she said, in a firm yet caring way, "You must go to Iona." This lodged deeply in my soul.

Edinburgh was an amazing place, beautiful in a different way. It had no heavy industry and lacked the pollution that was clearly evident in London and New York City. It was a center of government, culture and learning. Edinburgh was a clean, green and lovely city, where the arts and medicine thrived. Soon after I arrived, the Edinburgh Festival took place, with events at the castle on the hill and throughout the city. There were the main cultural events, including the largest group of the best bagpipers that I had ever heard. There was also the "Fringe" festival and "Beyond the Fringe." These avant-garde festivals consisted of exquisite music, drama, dance, and all kinds of art shows. I was in heaven, surrounded by culture, a welcome respite to my intense medical studies.

My stay abroad was a time of growth and development, both personally and professionally. I ended up traveling to the remote isle of Iona, where no cars were allowed. One day I swam in one of the beautiful bays with a solitary seal, who rubbed its body against mine. We then barked to each other. The trip was healing after the painful divorce. There was also a very memorable excursion to beautiful green Ireland with a lovely young woman who laughed uncontrollably when she had an orgasm.

I held a summer research fellowship in suicidology at the University of Edinburgh, in the Department of Psychiatry on the Morningside campus. My research advisor, Norman Kreitman, was a well-known epidemiologist in parasuicide and a published poet. He became a colleague and a friend, as well as a mentor in scientific research and poetry.

While in Edinburgh, I carried out a study of serious suicide attempts. The research involved eight hundred eighty-six patients. It was published in 1970, the year I graduated from medical school. I worked at the Royal Edinburgh Infirmary in the emergency department, where I went on rounds and had access to the records of patients who had attempted suicide.

When I think back on my time there, I marvel at my courage, the way I just jumped in and did it. This was before personal computers! The experience was profitable for me, and I learned how to be a humanistic physician-scientist. As Norman Cousins wrote in his foreword to *Medicine as a Human Experience*, "For ultimately it is our regard for the human soul that determines the worth of our science."[1]

After my stay in Edinburgh, I ventured to Croatia on a US Public Health Department fellowship to study the health care system of Yugoslavia at the University of Zagreb. Before President Kennedy's death, he arranged, as payment for war debt, for two medical students from every medical school in America to study socialized medicine in Yugoslavia. Most likely, he thought a cadre of future doctors would support universal health care. While in Zagreb, the fellows lived with families. My host was a widow who took in three medical students. I shared the upstairs with one of the other medical students, a former nun. We developed a loving relationship that contributed greatly to my healing.

When I returned to medical school, I had only six months left before I graduated. It was a special time, and I met a beautiful and bright nursing student named Debbie. I read something that she had written on ecology in the Student Health Organization Newsletter, and I asked her out for coffee in the cafeteria. She had been a cheerleader in high school, and her looks matched. We fell in love. Our relationship had a passionate beginning, and she spent a lot of time at my little red brick cottage. Debbie eventually became my second wife and the mother of my three daughters.

I was honored to speak at my graduation banquet. My topic was "Physician, Heal Thyself."[2] As a senior, I was also humbled by being elected to the Honor Medical Society, Alpha Omega Alpha. This was something that differentiated me from my father and got him to say that he was proud of me … a treasured moment in our relationship.

My internship in California would be one of the most tumultuous and stressful years of my life. It was fortunate then that Debbie stayed behind in Columbia to finish her senior year and become a registered nurse.

Something in the lake
dark moon blooms
a woman emerges

NOTES

1 See foreword, "Physician as Humanist" by Norman Cousins in *Medicine as a Human Experience*. David E. Reiser and David H. Rosen, *Medicine as a Human Experience* (Gaithersburg, MD: Aspen Publishers, Inc., 1985), xvi.

2 David H. Rosen, "Physician, Heal Thyself," *Clinical Medicine* 80 (1973): 25 27.

25

Intern in San Francisco

The physician strives for the good as the artist strives for the beautiful, each pushed on by that admirable feeling we call virtue.

HONORÉ DE BALZAC

Leaving the safety of Columbia, Missouri, and medical school for the reality of San Francisco, California, was an eye-opener. Little did I know that, during my first year as a medical doctor at San Francisco General Hospital (SFGH), I would treat all types of wounded individuals from the poorest to the wealthiest. I would also be part of a hospital workers' strike and a standoff with the police in the Emergency Room (ER) concerning the *Los Siete de la Raza*.[1] I was an intern through the University of California San Francisco (UCSF) at SFGH, where I would do my psychiatric residency at the Langley Porter Neuropsychiatric Institute.

My internship was necessary in order to get a medical license. It allowed me to practice being a real doctor with phenomenal supervision. In the hospital, I was assisted, if needed, by Faith Fitzgerald who was the Chief Resident in Medicine. She was extremely helpful and a great teacher. We were both Alpha Omega Alpha, so there was mutual respect. It was difficult, even traumatic, but we prevented patients from dying due to sudden heart attacks and bleeding ulcers.

INTERN

I loved psychiatry, which was the reason that I went to medical school, and I worked on the locked psychiatric wards. I recall a manic patient sweeping and mopping the floor repeatedly in order to be helpful. He also had it all worked out on paper how to make Los Angeles smog-free by launching the city's smog into space. He even contacted Governor Reagan's office to offer the plan to the state government at no expense. I'm still in touch with a female patient who was diagnosed as a paranoid schizophrenic. She recovered, and I saw her throughout my psychiatric residency and beyond. She is now a fine artist. Her lithograph of an angel currently hangs on a wall in our home.

Why did we go on strike? There were two main reasons. Firstly, the salary was so low that it was difficult to live in San Francisco. We made eight thousand dollars a year, and street cleaners made seventeen thousand dollars! Secondly, the vials of blood and urine samples sent to the lab often never got there, so we had to take them ourselves or ask medical students to do that chore. We wanted a decent wage for ourselves and the lab workers.

Working in the ER was a traumatic time. The ER was the most difficult rotation. We were on thirty-six hours and off twelve hours for a month. When I left my shift in the ER, I would get to my apartment on Green Street and collapse. When I woke up, I would eat and return. For my own healing, I wrote and painted. In one of my essays, a cardiovascular surgery resident says to a young woman who severed her radial artery and nearly died, "Next time why don't you jump off the Golden Gate Bridge?"[2]

I recall with amazement when the members of *Los Siete de la Raza*, suffering from gun shot wounds, were brought into the ER. In a matter of minutes, the place was teeming with police officers. They clogged the treatment rooms and hallways. I remember the head of the ER saying (with the staff's support) "Get out, or the next wounded police officer brought in will not be treated." Within a short amount of time, nearly all the police were gone. I recall later treating one of the *Los Siete* on a medical ward, while an armed police officer sat outside the door.

One day, I sewed up the head of Grace Slick, the lead singer of Jefferson Airplane, after she ran her car into a stone pillar at the entrance to the Golden Gate Bridge. She didn't stay long. Once she was medically stable, she was whisked out of SFGH and transferred to a private hospital by ambulance.

When I was rear-ended by an intoxicated doctor while stopped at a red light on my way back to SFGH, he left the scene of the accident. Luckily I got his license number. Two of my vertebral bodies were fractured, and I had to wear a neck brace for two months. It ironically turned out that he worked in an alcohol treatment facility in San Francisco.

I remember a beautiful young African American woman, dressed professionally, who was brought to the ER. The attendants said that they attempted to save her, but they were unable to do anything. She had a bullet hole in the center of her forehead. She was DOA (dead on arrival); this was the type of tragedy that I never got used to.

The holidays were a heartfelt occasion. Four of us formed a band and serenaded patients with Christmas carols. In retrospect it seems fitting that I played little Buddhist cymbals, while my fellow interns played a triangle and two guitars. The triangle along with the cymbals sounded like bells ringing. I'll never forget seeing the young and old patients experience joy in the hospital.

One of the oddest things during that year was a visit by Lynn on my birthday. I was expecting my sister Janet and her first husband, Bob, to take me to a performance by a renowned pianist, Van Cliburn. Lynn appeared before they arrived. She gave me a sand dollar and told me she was dating Dr David Rosen, a psychiatrist in nearby Marion County. He practiced primal scream therapy. I thanked her, but I was in such a state of shock that she left quickly. The truth is stranger than fiction!

By the end of the year, I was a real medical doctor, licensed by the state of California. I loved being a general physician so much that I even moonlighted (took weekend shifts as the only doctor) at Hillcrest Hospital in Petaluma during my residency. The extra money was helpful. Eventually, I did give it up and became a specialist in psychiatry.

While it had been difficult to be apart from Debbie, it was a blessing due to the fact that I had been working excessively and was exhausted most of the time. My political action and antiwar protesting took up my limited spare time. But I wanted to deepen my relationship with Debbie, so after my internship, Debbie came to San Francisco. We found an apartment on Twenty-First Street, and went on holiday at Yosemite National Park.

Billowing clouds
are ours —
adventure of love

NOTES

1 Seven young Latinos from the Mission District of San Francisco were called *Los Siete de la Raza*, meaning *seven of the race*, after a 1969 incident with police that resulted in an officer's death. However, all seven were acquitted.

2 David H. Rosen, "View from the Bridge," *Journal of the American Medical Association*, 254 (1985): 3314.

26

Becoming a Shrink

The care of the human mind
is the most noble branch of medicine.

HUGO GROTIUS

The first year of my psychiatric residency at the Langley Porter Neuropsychiatric Institute, in the Department of Psychiatry at UCSF, began on a locked ward with the most severely disturbed. The patients suffered from schizophrenia, suicidal depression, mania, and schizoaffective disorder.

I started out each morning crying in the parking lot. I cried for my war-wounded father, who today would have been diagnosed with Post-Traumatic Stress Disorder (PTSD) and schizophrenic reaction, paranoid type. Regardless of his psychiatric diagnoses, he received a Purple Heart. After being shipped back from the Pacific, on his way to Iwo Jima, he was hospitalized at Saint Elizabeth's in Bethesda, Maryland. My father received insulin coma shock treatments and eventually electroconvulsive therapy (ECT).

I sobbed early each morning because I had to arrive before rounds to give ECT to multiple patients. It seemed like a primitive treatment. Electrical currents were passed through the brain that prompted grand mal seizures. Fortunately, oxygen and muscle relaxants were given to prevent memory loss and injury from the seizures. The therapy was typically administered three times per week for four weeks. In spite of its reputation, the results were positive, and I saw treatment-resistant psychotics, especially the suicidally depressed, become well. This is no surprise: research before and after ECT revealed that the neurotransmitters in the cerebral spinal fluid increased after the treatment. This controversial technique, so criticized in *One Flew Over the Cuckoo's Nest*,[1] was developed by the Nobel Laureate in Medicine Dr Ugo Cerletti. He observed that psychotic (schizophrenic and/or suicidal) epileptic patients recovered after a series of grand mal seizures.

Despite this knowledge, being a sensitive soul, each time I assisted in administering shock therapy I cried internally: grown men and psychiatrists did not outwardly cry. I'm sure others noticed my melancholic nature. Nevertheless, my temperament served me well, as it enabled me to empathize with my patients and my father.

One of my patients was a young woman who had killed her baby with carbon monoxide, in an unsuccessful suicide attempt. Another psychotic woman was brought in by her family when she began washing lettuce with Lysol, to remove the germs, before preparing sandwiches for lunch. And then there was the man who couldn't drive across the Golden Gate Bridge, because he was afraid he would stop and jump off. Another woman believed that she had a radio implanted in her pelvis by her obstetrician.

My second rotation was on the youth ward, which I liked very much. My negative father complex ,however, left me with a lack of authoritativeness, and all of my adolescent patients acted out at the same time. One escaped, another used drugs and a third attempted suicide. A fourth adolescent was sexually inappropriate with the head nurse, who was married to the head of the ward, Dr Fari Amini. Dr Amini called me in and said that I needed to see a Freudian analyst: he was one himself. It was clear that I needed help, as all of my patients were out of control. I told him that I would see a Jungian but not a Freudian. I saw Jung as maternal and Freud as patriarchal. I had always favored my mother and women; I'm sure some folks would have described me as a ladies' man. Nevertheless, wise Dr Amini advised me to see the most Jungian of the Freudian analysts and the most Freudian of the Jungians, and then decide. I agreed and saw Dr Fred Alston (the Freudian) and Dr Donald Sandner (the Jungian). I used a dream in the literal, Talmudic sense to decide who to see. I dreamt that I returned to Dr Alston, so I chose him. I ended up liking Dr Alston, and I saw him for nearly four years. He facilitated an in-depth therapeutic experience for me concerning my father complex. I also learned to set clear boundaries with others.

Seeing Dr Alston was a "blue experience" for me. Everything in his office was blue velvet: the chairs, the couch and even the curtains. I felt like I'd entered a cave of melancholy. The main thing that I remember from this period of analytic psychotherapy is that setting limits is a sign of mental health. During this time, I committed psychic murder of a disguised image of my father through a dream: the cold-blooded murder of a mafia leader. This was at the root of my self-destructive behavior and my problem with authority.

While I was seeing Dr Alston, I carried out research on survivors who jumped off the Golden Gate Bridge. It was during this study that I coined the term *egocide*. I realized that the death of the ego, or suicidal self, is a meaningful alternative to suicide.

During the first year of my psychiatric residency, we had mandatory weekly group training sessions. The meetings were led by Denny Zeitlin, a gifted therapist and Jazz musician. Everything I learned about group therapy began in these sessions. As a result of this experience, I co-led art therapy groups and some for suicide attempters. An benefit of the art therapy groups was the use of creative arts as healing agents.

I became life-long friends with Alice Tamura, who planted a seed by giving me *In Praise of Shadows* by Junichiro Tanizaki. This seed grew into a love of Japan: its people, nature and culture—and especially a love of haiku poetry.

I am a spiritual person, and have always gravitated toward Taoism and Buddhism. Perhaps this is why I am a Jungian analyst.[2] I've known that there is something beyond the ego, whether it be the Self (Jung), the Tao (Taoism) or nothing (Buddhism). When I read Jung's *Memories, Dreams, Reflections*, Lao Tzu's *Tao Te Ching*, and later Rodger Kamenetz's *The Jew in the Lotus*, I felt at home. I completed the first year of psychiatric training feeling competent in dealing with psychotic individuals. Increasingly, I knew that the ego was a barrier to relating to and with the Ultimate or, as Spinoza called it, the Eternal One.

Buddhism —
no ego or self
to kill

NOTES

1 Ken Kesey, *One Flew Over the Cuckoo's Nest* (New York: New American Library, 1962).

2 David H. Rosen, "The Evolution of a Jungian Shaman: A Conversation with David H. Rosen" (Interviewed by Joel Weishaus), *Shamanic Applications Review*, no. 7 (1999): 29-35.

27

Going In-Depth with the Wounded Well

The patient should be educated to liberate and fulfill his own nature, not to resemble ourselves.

SIGMUND FREUD
The Standard Edition of the Complete Psychological Works of Sigmund Freud, Volume 17

My second year of psychiatric training was with neurotic outpatients, and I continued to see a few severely disturbed patients. I knew, as did Frieda Fromm-Reichmann, Clifford Beers and John Perry, that psychotic patients could recover. After all, my father was a living example. Langley Porter Institute was in San Francisco, so we had superb supervisors. They were mainly Freudians. This was the nature of the beast at the time. Psychiatry was mostly talking therapy, with some use of medication. Today, the discipline has sadly become basically a biological and medication-oriented specialty.

Amidst the Freudians, there were a few Jungians. I was exposed to the psychologies of Freud and Jung as an undergraduate, so I was thrilled to be working with both. Under the supervision of Freudian and Jungian analysts, I learned to value the healing doctor-patient relationship.[1] Transference and counter-transference seemed logical to me.[2] While I respected Freud's views, the question of meaning and purpose drew me to the existential and humanistic nature of Jung's psychology. Because I favor the spiritual and cosmic aspects of reality, Jung's views on evolution were more harmonious with my nature and helped me to focus beyond the personal. Jung's archetypes and the collective unconscious, as I would later write in other books, such as *The Tao of Jung* and *The Tao of Elvis*, made sense to me. Since I have experienced the death of the ego, combining Jung's insight with Taoism and Buddhism has been the most realistic path for me, personally and professionally.[3]

YOUNG PSYCHIATRIST

During my second year, I began teaching medical students, and I came to love it. During my residency, I emphasized ethics and the value of clear boundaries with both patients and students. I taught with Mardi Horowitz, a psychiatrist and Freudian-trained analyst. He became an outstanding mentor for my teaching, research and clinical work. Mardi was also a painter, who was not afraid to display his work. He was quite personable. On occasion, he invited me to his home. In a real way, he was a positive father figure for me.

An important ethical issue occurred in a group of medical students that I was teaching. A very attractive female student started flirting with me. My response, which I have adhered to in all of my professional relationships, was to refrain from crossing that boundary.[4] I arranged to have the young woman transferred to another section. This has been a constant ethic for me: no sexual relationships with students or patients, period.

My favorite supervisor was Fari Amini, who was originally a mathematician from Iran. Aside from his work on the youth ward, he also served as a forensic consultant who evaluated murderers at San Quentin Prison. He was brilliant and compassionate in his own detached way. I will never forget learning about Freud's "pain and pleasure principle." This was vividly illustrated to me when I witnessed Fari place two fingers carefully around an eyebrow hair and yank it out without wincing. Many years later Fari coauthored an exceptional volume on love.[5] Heraclitus's concept of *enantiodromia*, everything goes to the opposite, is so true.[6]

Given my own blessing of love with my wife, Lanara, I recall Rumi's words: In your light I learn how to love. / In your beauty, how to make poems. / You dance inside my chest, / where no one sees you, / but sometimes I do, / and that light becomes this art.[7]

My experiences taught me that neurotic conflict, in a period of emotional upheaval, often leads to the discovery of meaning. As I was immersed in my own in-depth Freudian therapy, I found that my dreams were exceptionally helpful. For example, while seeing Dr Alston and studying my negative shadow, my father complex, I confronted and killed father figures in my dreams. Marion Woodman uses the term *psychic murder*.[8] I use the terms *egocide* and *shadowcide*. I underwent an inner killing of the self-destructive part of my ego or false self. As I have discovered personally and professionally, egocide leads to a death-rebirth experience, so that one's true self can be actualized.

I felt helped by my dreams, so I began to ask my patients about their dreams. Usually dreams reveal deep affect surrounding personal issues, often beginning with mother-and-father conflicts. Yet I felt that Freud's reductionist view allowed one to blame one's parents. Jung's approach delved beyond one's parents to an evolutionary consideration of mothers and fathers, which is archetypal and collective.

I began to realize that one could re-parent oneself through loving inner father and mother archetypes. This re-parenting allows one to develop one's authentic self. Our grandfathers and grandmothers embody these archetypes. We share collective emotional experiences with these historical figures. Each day I pray to these ancestors, and I work hard to maintain a connection to these ancient parts of myself.

It was deep exploration within that allowed me to learn that I did not have to be caught up in the pain of my father's rage and war wounds. I also learned that I did not have to be snared in the smothering web of my mother's love. I found out, through painstaking work, that I could go through repeated death and rebirth phenomena and slowly become my real self.

My identity as a physician-specialist crystallized toward the end of my second year of residency. I wanted to be a husband and father as well. Living with Debbie, we often discussed the meaning of our lives. According to her mother, we were living in sin. She wouldn't even talk to Debbie on the phone. However, her father accepted her free spirit. Her mother's silence acted as a stressful pressure to get married. Being cut off from her mother for nearly two years negatively affected Debbie. I remember that she cried because of it.

We were both working a lot during this time.

I was distracted and moody while my ego was pumped up and down by my successes and failures in academia. My time was spent caring for my patients, preparing to teach, and reading multiple papers for seminars. Debbie was occupied with nursing and studying for a Masters in Ecology at San Francisco State. She worked and studied hard and was competitive with me. She spoke of getting a PhD in Clinical Psychology, which I supported.

In spite of everything, we were in love and discussed getting married and having children. As my second year ended, we decided to exchange rings. This decision brought Debbie into contact with her mother again. The two of them planned the big event for June 30, 1973. We were married in her mother's Presbyterian church. My parents attended, and my brother Bill was the best man.

Through the pines
full moon
rises

NOTES

1 David H. Rosen, "Inborn Basis for the Doctor Patient Relationship," *The Pharos* 55 (1992), 17, 21.

2 David H.Rosen, Foreword to Jan Wiener's *The Therapeutic Relationship: Transference, Countertransference and the Making of Meaning* (College Station: Texas A & M University Press, 2009).

3 David H. Rosen, "The Tao of Medicine," *The Pharos* 63 (2000), 14.

4 Peter Rutter, *Sex in the Forbidden Zone: When Men in Power–Therapists, Doctors, Clergy, Teachers, and Others –Betray Women's Trust* (Los Angeles: J.P. Tarcher, 1989).

5 Thomas Lewis, Fari Amini, and Richard Lannon, *A General Theory of Love* (New York: Random House, 2000).

6 Jung uses this term frequently in his writings. For example, see Carl Jung, *The Archetypes and the Collective Unconscious*, Volume 9, trans. R.F.C. Hull (Princeton, NJ: Princeton University Press, 1990), 229.

7 Jelaluddin Rumi, *The Essential Rumi: New Expanded Edition*, trans. Coleman Barks (San Francisco: HarperCollins Publishers, 2010), 122.

8 See Marion Woodman, *The Owl was a Baker's Daughter: Obesity, Anorexia Nervosa and the Repressed Feminine* (Toronto: Inner City Books, 1980), 120.

28

A Second Marriage and my Father's Death

It is indeed high time for the clergyman and the psychotherapist to join forces.

CARL JUNG

Modern Man in Search of a Soul

I was twenty-eight when I entered my third year of psychiatric residency. Getting married pulled me toward maturity. I received a National Institute of Mental Health (NIMH) research fellowship at the University of Edinburgh, so we ended up going to Edinburgh for our honeymoon. The wedding went well, but it was the last time I saw my father alive.

In an interesting contrast to my spiritual orientation, Debbie and I lived in a minister's home in Edinburgh, which we found through the University Housing office. We lived there from July through October, while I completed my scheduled research project. The study was a five-year follow-up investigation of the serious suicide attempters whom I had studied during medical school.[1]

I worked with Dr Norman Kreitman again in the Psychiatry Department at the University of Edinburgh. The Kreitmans became a second family to us. Dr Kreitman became a surrogate father figure. As I mentioned earlier, he was also a poet.[2] Now I had an academic physician-scientist mentor who blended art and science.

Edinburgh was a great place for newlyweds. Lovely green parks, marvelous culture and our love kept us occupied. In sum, we were happy.

MARRIAGE TO DEBBIE

The joy became sorrow on October 27, 1973. I received a phone call in the middle of the night; Debbie answered the telephone. She said, "It's your mother." I could tell that something was wrong. My mother, who had divorced my father for the second time a month earlier, was abrupt. She said matter-of-factly, "I have some bad news." She paused and then said, "Your father died instantly in a head-on automobile collision. The funeral will be in ten days." I was in shock; stunned into disbelief and silence. I managed to say that we would return for the funeral, then said good-bye to my mother. Debbie went back to sleep in the enormous four-poster bed, but I just sat there staring off into the darkness.

Then something occurred for the first and only time in my life. I saw Jesus Christ in the upper left corner of the room. I recall finding it comforting. There was light in the darkness. Two years later, I read in William James' *The Varieties of Religious Experience* that such a vision was not uncommon among spiritual individuals going through a traumatic event.[3] Carl Jung saw Jesus as an archetype of the Self or divine wholeness.[4]

My born-again sister Janet rejoiced when I told her about this apparition. I, however, recalled how my father, born and raised an orthodox Jew, was put off by Janet's marriage to a fundamentalist Christian. During the wedding, he inadvertently stepped on her train and momentarily halted the procession.

I also remember exiting the Baptist church with my father before the reception started. He headed to the parking lot and opened the trunk of his rental car to retrieve a cold bottle of champagne. I will never forget his delight as he popped the cork and poured the champagne into paper cups, and then we toasted. He said, "You can't have a wedding without a celebratory drink." After we finished the bottle, we returned to the reception where alcohol was not allowed.

Although happily married, I was profoundly grief-stricken. I was so distraught that I started smoking and drinking again, habits I had given up in medical school. I had new self-destructive behavior to work on with Dr Alston.

We returned for the funeral in early November.

I was pleased that my father's oldest sister Frimi, and his two younger identical twin sisters, Ruth and Esta, were there. Sam Silverman, my father's best childhood friend and my godfather, was also in attendance. Sam's presence comforted me, as I mourned the death of my father at such a young age.

My father, at age sixty-five, was buried in the Jewish cemetery in Springfield, Missouri. The rabbi said the Kaddish as my dad was lowered into his final resting place. We planted a maple tree by his grave site. It's quite beautiful now in the fall, the season of his passing. We all cried during the ceremony.

Sam told me later that my father was a great physician and artist. He said that the war changed my father, but he was resilient. He continued to work hard and paint. My dad was able to recover from his war wounds and be a good doctor and father. He even supported my own conscientious objection to war.

I have always thought that my father missed the best years of his life. This wisdom came from his father Abraham (or Pop), who lived to be ninety-seven. Pop once told me that the sunset years (seventy to ninety) were the best.

After a somber holiday season (Thanksgiving, Christmas and Hanukkah), the new year was a rebirth of sorts. I did a rotation with severely disturbed children on a locked ward.

My work with the troubled kids sparked a new-found compassion deep within me. My inner child was wounded again and sympathy turned into empathy. The first time I felt such pain was during my infancy, when my disturbed father returned from WW II. Now I emerged as a caring doctor who helped traumatized children and their parents with difficult, but rewarding, healing experiences.

Flowers grow and
leaves fall —
Nature's way

NOTES

1 David H. Rosen, "The Serious Suicide Attempt: A Five Year Follow up Study of 886 Patients," *Journal of the American Medical Association* 235 (1976): 2105, 2109.

2 Norman Kreitman, *Dancing in the Dark: New and Selected Poems* (Edinburgh: Lauder Press, 2010).

3 William James, *The Varieties of Religious Experience* (New York: Penguin Books, 1982).

4 Michael F Palmer, *Freud and Jung on Religion* (London: Routledge, 1997), 135.

29

Searching and Researching

Never lose a holy curiosity.

ALBERT EINSTEIN
to William Miller,
as quoted in *Life* magazine,
May 2, 1955

When I turned twenty-nine in 1974, I was asked to be Chief Resident at the Langley Porter Institute. I knew that this year would be about testing the academic waters to see if I could float and swim. The year also allowed me to decide if I wanted that kind of life. The faculty, in turn, assessed whether or not I was a suitable addition: previous chief residents often became staff.

My duties were to help run the residency program, teach and conduct original research. I also learned to become an administrator of sorts. I taught and mentored psychiatric residents and the first and second-year medical students.

My research project involved interviews with survivors who jumped off the Golden Gate Bridge. While deciding what aspect of suicide to study, I read a story on the front page of the *San Francisco Chronicle* about a Stanford University student who survived a suicidal jump. The article said that there were others who had also survived previous jumps. (Interestingly, physicists have deemed that it is impossible to survive the two hundred fifty foot drop). I found and interviewed a total of ten survivors.[1] The study helped me understand what happens in suicide, and that egocide is a meaningful alternative to killing oneself.

During this time, I also co-wrote a successful NIMH grant proposal with my wife. The idea for the project was hatched in Edinburgh, when we learned that the tiny and remote Shetland Islands in the North Sea were set to become the home of Europe's largest oil port. During our time in Scotland, we visited the Shetland Islands and realized that it was a perfect "experiment in nature"! Heretofore, the largest industry on the islands was a twenty-person fish processing plant. Our research project, "Shetland Health," consisted of studying the impact of the North Sea oil development on physical and mental health.

Both the Golden Gate Bridge survivors research study and the Shetland investigation project launched my career in academic medicine and psychiatry. In addition, I published my first book in 1974 and received my first grant the next year. The foundation was laid for my becoming a professor.

As Chief Resident, I learned more about teaching and discovered how well it suited me. I also enjoyed research. It was during this year that I realized that "research is me-search." My survival of a suicidal crisis primed me to go deeper. The survivors study taught me that I, too, had gone through egocide and transformation.

I got the idea for this new term *egocide* from one of the survivors who said, "Dr Rosen, the identity that drove me to the Golden Gate Bridge, parked my car, wrote a suicide note, walked out to the first suspension tower, and leapt, *died*." I knew that the term *failed suicide* made no sense. I also understood that the ego identity, the suicidal self that precipitated the leap off the bridge, was killed the way a serpent sheds its skin. It was amazing to witness the resulting transformation of despair to hope. By preserving our authentic selves, we can become more altruistic and find purpose for our lives.

My findings from this project, modeled after William James, became the basis for an innovative in-depth treatment for suicidal individuals.[2]

William James, the physician and founder of American psychology and philosophy, was an exemplary figure for my own work. He outlined a "neurology of religion."[3] What has transpired over many years is a neuroscience of spiritual attributes related to altruism, virtue, peace, and compassion.[4]

I found that egocide opened doors to creativity and healing. The false self that was hell-bent on self-destructive behavior dies, and the true self is reborn.[5] Clearly, the death of my suicidal self enabled me to join art and science in my personal and professional life. I believe that creative change is the key to transforming suicidal depression into self-actualization.

Searching
researching
light in the abyss

NOTES

1 David H. Rosen, "Suicide Survivors: A Follow-up Study of Persons Who Survived Jumping From the Golden Gate and San Francisco-Oakland Bay Bridges," *Western Journal of Medicine* 122 (1975): 289-294. Initially there were six, but later I interviewed four more. See *Transforming Depression* (2002).

2 David H. Rosen, *Transforming Depression: Healing the Soul through Creativity* (York Beach, ME: Nicolas-Hays, 2002).

3 See William James, *The Varieties of Religious Experience* (Rockville, MD: Arc Manor Publishers, 2008), 11-27.

4 See Antonio R. Damasio, *Looking for Spinoza: Joy, Sorrow, and the Feeling Brain* (Orlando, FL: Harcourt, 2003) and George E. Vaillant, *Spiritual Evolution: A Scientific Defense of Faith* (New York: Broadway Books, 2008).

5 See D.W. Winnicott, "Fear of Breakdown" in *The British School of Psychoanalysis: The Independent Tradition*, ed. Gregorio Kohon (New Haven: Yale University Press, 1986), 173-182.

Bibliography

Abrams, James. "Hail in the Begging Bowl: The Odyssey and Poetry of Santoka." *Monumenta Nipponica*, 32 (1997): 301.

Anderson, Charles M. and Marian MacCurdy, eds. *Writing & Healing: Toward an Informed Practice*. Urbana, IL: National Council of Teachers of English, 2000.

Barks, Coleman, trans., with John Moyne, A.J. Arberry and Reynold Nicholson. *The Essential Rumi*. San Francisco: HarperSanFrancisco, 1995.

Basho, Matsuo. *Basho's Narrow Road: Narrow Road to the Interior*. Translated by Hiroaki Sato. Berkeley, CA: Stone Bridge Press, 1996.

Beers, Clifford W. *A Mind that Found Itself: An Autobiography*. Pittsburgh, PA: University of Pittsburgh Press, 1981.

Bergson, Henri. *Creative Evolution*. Translated by Arthur Mitchell. New York: Henry Holt & Company, 1911.

Blake, William. *Songs of Innocence and Experience*. Princeton, NJ: William Blake Trust/Princeton University, 1991.

Blos, Peter. "The Place of the Adolescent Process in the Analysis of the Adult." *The Psychoanalytic Study of the Child*, 44 (1989): 3-18.

Bly, Robert, James Hillman and Michael Meade. "Two Poems by Rumi." In *The Rag and Bone Shop of the Heart*. New York: HarperCollins, 1992.

Buber, Martin. *I and Thou*. New York: Charles Scribner's Sons, 1970.

Camus, Albert. *The Myth of Sisyphus*. New York: Vintage Books, 1955.

Chardin, Teilhard de. *The Future of Man*. New York: Harper & Row, 1964.

Chekhov, Anton Pavlovich. *The Essential Tales of Chekhov*. Hopewell, NJ: Ecco Press, 1998.

Churchill, Winston. "The Russian Enigma." *BBC*, October 1, 1939.

Cicero, Julie. *Waking up Alone: Grief and Healing*. Bloomington, IN: AuthorHouse, 2007.

Connolly, Julian W. *Nabokov and his Fiction: New Perspectives*. New York: Cambridge University Press, 1999.

Damasio, Antonio R. *Looking for Spinoza: Joy, Sorrow, and the Feeling Brain*. Orlando, FL: Harcourt, 2003.

Dewey, John. *Experience and Education*. New York: Macmillan, 1938.

Dickinson, Emily. *Emily Dickinson*. Edited by Frances Schoonmaker Bolin. New York: Sterling Publishing Co., 1994.

Dossey, Larry. *Healing Words: The Power of Prayer and the Practice of Medicine*. New York: Harper Collins, 1993.

Dostoevsky, Fyodor. *Memoirs from the House of the Dead*. New York: Oxford University Press, 2001.

Durrell, Lawrence. *Bitter Lemons*. New York: Dutton, 1957.

Dylan, Bob. *Chronicles*. New York: Simon & Schuster, 2004.

Einstein, Albert. *Albert Einstein, the Human Side: New Glimpses from Archives*. Edited by Helen Dukas and Banesh Hoffmann. Princeton, NJ: Princeton University Press, 1979.

Eliot, T.S. *Collected Poems, 1909-1962*. New York: Harcourt, Brace & World, 1963.

Emerson, Ralph Waldo. *Journals of Ralph Waldo Emerson: With Annotations*, Volume 6. Edited by Edward Waldo Emerson and Waldo Emerson Forbes. Boston: Houghton Mifflin, 1911.

Erikson, Erik. *Life Cycle Completed*. New York: W.W. Norton, 1982.

Ferlinghetti, Lawrence. *Endless Life: Selected Poems*. New York: New Directions, 1981.

Frankl, Viktor. *Man's Search for Meaning: An Introduction to Logotherapy*. New York: Simon & Schuster, 1984.

Freud, Sigmund. *The Interpretation of Dreams*. New York: Basic Books, 1955.

—. *The Standard Edition of the Complete Psychological Works of Sigmund Freud*, Volume 17. London: Hogarth Press, 1966-74.

Fromm-Reichmann, Frieda. *Principles of Intensive Psychotherapy*. Chicago: Chicago University Press, 1950.

Ginsberg, Alan. *Howl and Other Poems*. San Francisco: City Lights Books, 1959.

Goethe, Johann Wolfgang von. *The Sorrows of Young Werther*. New York: Random House, 1971.

Hanson, William. *Smart Medicine: How the*

Changing Role of Doctors will Revolutionize Health Care. New York: Palgrave Macmillan, 2011.

Hendricks, Gay and Laura Joyce. *A Year of Living Consciously: 365 Daily Inspirations for Creating a Life of Passion and Purpose*. New York: Harper Collins, 1998.

Hesse, Hermann. *Siddhartha*. New York: New Directions, 1951.

Higgins, Patrick. *Before Elvis There Was Nothing*. New York: Carroll and Graf, 1994.

Hillel, et al. *The Sayings of the Jewish Fathers (PirkeAboth)*.Translated by W.O.E.Oesterley. New York: The Macmillan Company, 1919.

Hillman, James. *Betrayal*. London: Guild of Pastoral Psychology, 1964.

Holmes Sr., Oliver Wendell. *The Professor at the Breakfast Table*. London, J. M. Dent, 1906.

Huxley, Aldous. *A Brave New World*. New York: Harper Collins, 1932.

—. *Complete Essays: 1920-1925*. Chicago: I.R. Dee, 2000.

Jacobi, Jolande, ed., Norbert Guterman, trans. *Paracelsus: Selected Writings*. Princeton, NJ: Princeton University Press, 1995.

James, William. *The Varieties of Religious Experience*. New York: Penguin Books, 1982.

Joyce, James. *Ulysses*. New York: Random House, 1946.

Jung, Carl. *The Archetypes and the Collective Unconscious*, Volume 9. Translated by R.F.C. Hull. Princeton, NJ: Princeton University Press, 1990.

—. *Contributions to Analytical Psychology*. New York: Harcourt, Brace and Co., 1928.

—. *Memories, Dreams, Reflections*. New York: Pantheon, 1963.

—. *Modern Man in Search of a Soul*. Great Britain: Routledge, 2005.

—. "The Nature and Activity of the Psyche." In *The Collected Works of C.G.Jung*. Bollingen Series 20, Volume 14. Princeton, NJ: Princeton University Press, 1969.

Kabat-Zinn, Jon. *Wherever You Go, There You Are: Mindfulness Meditation in Everyday Life*. New York: Hyperion, 1994.

Kafka, Franz. *The Trial*. New York: Schocken Books, 1968.

Kamenetz, Rodger. *The Jew in the Lotus: A Poet's Rediscovery of Jewish Identity in Buddhist India.* San Francisco: HarperSanFrancisco, 1994.

Keats, John. *Selected Poems and Letters*. London: Oxford University Press, 1964.

Kesey, Ken. *One Flew Over the Cuckoo's Nest*. New York: New American Library, 1962.

Lao Tzu. *Tao Te Ching*. Translated by Steven Mitchell. New York: HarperCollins, 1988.

—.1992. *Hua Hu Ching* (The Unknown Teachings of Lao Tzu). Translated by B. Walker. HarperSanFrancisco (a division of HarperCollins).

Lawrence, D. H. *Lady Chatterley's Lover*. New York: Grove Press, 1993.

Levey, Joel and Michelle Levey. *The Fine Arts of Relaxation, Concentration, and Meditation: Ancient Skills for Modern Minds.* Boston: Wisdom Publications, 2003.

Levinas, Emmanuel. *Ethics and Infinity*. Translated by Philippe Nemo. Pittsburgh, PA: Duquesne University Press, 1985.

Lewis, Thomas, Fari Amini and Richard Lannon. *A General Theory of Love*. New York: Random House, 2000.

Mann, Thomas. *The Magic Mountain: A Novel*. New York: A. Knopf, 1995.

Marrs, Suzanne. *Eudora Welty: A Biography.* Orlando, FL: Harcourt, 2005.

Maslow, Abraham. *Religions, Values and Peak-Experiences*. New York: Viking Press, 1970.

Maugham, William Somerset. *The Complete Short Stories of W. Sommerset Maugham*. Garden City, NY: Doubleday, 1952.

McMillan, Frank. *Finding Jung: Frank N. McMillan, Jr, A Life in Quest of the Lion*. College Station, TX: Texas A&M University Press, 2012.

Miller, Arthur. *Timebends: A Life*. London: Minerva, 1990.

Miller, Henry. *The Colossus of Maroussi*. New York: New Directions, 1941.

Miller, William. "Death of a Genius: His Fourth Dimension, Time, Overtakes Einstein." *LIFE*, May 2, 1955, p 62. Ming-Dao. Deng. *Everyday Tao: Living with Balance and Harmony*. San Francisco:

HarperSanFrancisco, 1996.

Menninger, Karl. *Man Against Himself*. New York: Harcourt, Brace, 1938.

Montaigne, Michel de. *Selected Essays of Michel de Montaigne*. New York: T. Y. Crowell and Co., 1903.

Nabokov, Vladimir Vladimirovich. *Speak, Memory: An Autobiography Revisited*. New York: Putnam, 1966.

Nakagawa, Soen. *Endless Vow: The Zen Path of Soen Nakagawa*. Translated and edited by Kazuaki Tanahashi and Sherry Chayat. Boston: Shambhala Publications, 1996.

Nin, Anais. *Henry and June: From the Unexpurgated Diary of Anais Nin*. San Diego: Harcourt Brace Jovanovich, 1986.

Osler, William. *Aequanimitas*. Philadelphia: Blakiston, 1932.

Patchen, Kenneth. *The Collected Poems of Kenneth Patchen*. New York: New Directions Publishing Corp., 1968.

Pennebaker, James W. *Emotion, Disclosure, and Health*. Washington, DC: American Psychological Association, 1995

—. *Opening Up: The Healing Power ofConfiding in Others*. New York: Morrow, 1990.

Perry, John W. *The Self in Psychotic Process, its Symbolization in Schizophrenia.* Forward by Carl Jung. Berkeley, CA: University of California Press, 1953.

Piozzi, Hester Lynch. *Anecdotes of the Late Samuel Johnson, LL.D (1786)*. New York: Garland Pub., 1974.

Plato. *The Republic*. Translated by Tom Griffith. Cambridge: Cambridge University Press, 2000.

Rilke, Rainer Maria. *The Selected Poetry of Rainer Maria Rilke*. New York: Random House, 1982.

Roberts, Elizabeth and Elias Amidon, eds. *Life Prayers From Around the World: 365 Prayers, Blessings, and Affirmations to Celebrate the Human Journey.* New York: Harper Collins, 1996.

Rosen, David H. “Conception: The Tao is Operating.” *Frogpond* 31.3 (2008): 49.

—. “Depression and Suicide.” In *Open Questions in Analytical Psychology*, edited by Mary Ann Mattoon, 612-619.Einsiedeln, Switzerland: Daimon Verlag, 1997.

—. *Henry's Tower*. Pittsford, NY: Platypus Books, 1984.

—. *Lesbianism: A Study of Female Homosexuality*. Springfield, IL: Charles Thomas Publisher, 1974.

—. "Physician, Heal Thyself." *Clinical Medicine* 80 (1973): 25-27.

—. "Scent of spring …". *Modern Haiku* 38.1 (2007): 67.

—. "The Serious Suicide Attempt: A Five Year Follow-up Study of 886 Patients." *Journal of the American Medical Association* 235 (1976): 2105-2109.

—. "Suicide Survivors: A Follow-up Study of Persons Who Survived Jumping From the Golden Gate and San Francisco-Oakland Bay Bridges." *Western Journal of Medicine*, 122 (1975): 289-294.

—. *The Tao of Elvis*. San Diego: Harcourt, 2002. 2nd ed. Pittsboro, NC: Rosenberry Books, 2012; Eugene, OR: Wipf & Stock, 2013.

—. *The Tao of Jung: The Way of Integrity*. New York: Arkana/Penguin,1997.

—. *Transforming Depression: A Jungian Approach Using the Creative Arts*. New York: Taucher/Putman, 1993.

—. *Transforming Depression: Healing the Soul through Creativity*. 2nd ed. New York: Arkana/ Penguin Group, 1996 and 3rd ed. York Beach, ME: Nicolas-Hays, 2002.

—. Transforming Depression Through Egocide." In *Sacred Sorrows: Embracing and Transforming Depression*, edited by John E. Nelson and Andrea Nelson, 198-213. New York: Taucher/Putman, 1997.

—. "View from the bridge." *Journal of the American Medical Association*, 254 (1985): 3314.

Rosen, David H. and Michael C. Luebbert, eds. 1999. *Evolution of the Psyche*. Westport,CT: Praeger.

Rosen, David H. and David E. Reiser. *Medicine as a Human Experience*. Gaithersburg, MD: Aspen Publishers, Inc., 1985.

Rosen, David H. Steven M. Smith, Holly L.

Huston, and Gilbert Gonzalez. "Empirical Study of Associations Between Symbols and Their Meanings: Evidence of Collective Unconscious(Archetypal) Memory." *Journal of Analytical Psychology* 36 (1991): 211-228.

Rosen, David H., and Joel Weishaus. "The Evolution of a Jungian Shaman: A Conversation with David H. Rosen." *Shamanic Applications Review*, 1999.

—. *The Healing Spirit of Haiku*. Berkeley, CA: North Atlantic Books, 2004.

Rosenzweig, Franz. *Understanding the Sick and the Healthy*. Translated by Nahum Glatzer. Cambridge, MA: Harvard University Press, 1999.

Rutter, Peter. *Sex in the Forbidden Zone: When Men in Power — Therapists, Doctors, Clergy, Teachers, and Others — Betray Women's Trust*. Los Angeles: J.P. Tarcher, 1989.

Salinger, J. D. *Catcher in the Rye*. Boston: Little, Brown, 1945.

Shakespeare, William. *Hamlet*. New York: Penguin, 2005.

Soeng, Mu. *Trust in Mind: The Rebellion of Chinese Zen*. Somerville, MA: Wisdom Publications, 2004.

Solnit, Rebecca. *A Field Guide to Getting* Lost. New York: Viking, 2005.

Soyinka, Wole. *You Must Set Forth at Dawn: A Memoir.* New York: Random House, 2006.

Spinoza, Benedictus de. *Ethics*. New York: Oxford University Press, 2000.

Stowe, Harriet Beecher. *The Pearl of Orr's Island: A Story of the Coast of Maine*. Boston: Houghton, Mifflin, 1896.

Taylor, Robert B. *White Coat Tales: Medicine's Heroes, Heritage and Misadventures*. New York: Springer Science and Business Media, LLC, 2008.

Thomas, Dylan. *The Poems of Dylan Thomas*. New York: New Directions Publishing Corp., 1971.

Thomas, Sam. *Bits & Snatches: The Selected Work of Sam Thomas*. Edited by Joel Weishaus. Brooklyn, NY: White Rose Press, 1974.

Tolstoy, Leo. *Anna Karenina: A Novel in*

Eight Parts. New York: Viking, 2001.

T'san, Seng. *The Book of Nothing: A Song of Enlightenment*. Translated by Phillip Dunn and Peter Jourdan. Kansas City, MO: Andrews McMeel Publishing, 2002.

Vaillant, George E. *Spiritual Evolution: A Scientific Defense of Faith*. New York: Broadway Books, 2008.

Watts, Alan. *The Way of Zen*. New York: Random House, 1957.

Welty, Eudora. *One Writer's Beginnings*. Cambridge, MA: Harvard University Press, 1998.

Wheelis, Allen. *How People Change*. New York: Harper & Row, 1973.

Whitman, Walt. *Leaves of Grass*. New York: New York University Press, 1965.

Whittier, John Greenleaf. *The Poetical Works of John Greenleaf Whittier*. Boston: Houghton, Mifflin and Co., 1892.

Wiener, Jan. *The Therapeutic Relationship: Transference, Countertransference and the Making of Meaning*. College Station, TX: Texas A & M University Press, 2009.

Williams, William Carlos. *The Autobiography of William Carlos Williams*. New York: Random House, 1951.

Winnicott, D.W. "Fear of Breakdown." In *The British School of Psychoanalysis: The Independent Tradition*, edited by Gregorio Kohon, 173-182. New Haven, CT: Yale University Press, 1986.

Woodman, Marion. *The Owl Was a Baker's Daughter: Obesity, Anorexia Nervosa and the Repressed Feminine*. Toronto: Inner City Books, 1980.

Woodward, Ralph. *Silverfish & Slate Pencils*. Christchurch, New Zealand:Cygnet, 2005.

Yang, Xianyi and Gladys Yang, trans. *Poetry and Prose of the Tang and Song*. Beijing, China: Panda Books, 2005.

Yeats, W. B. *The Collected Poems of W. B. Yeats*. New York: MacMillan, 1956.

About the Author

Dr David H. Rosen is a physician, psychiatrist, and Jungian analyst. The his interests include: finding meaning in suffering; spirituality as it relates to healing; dreams; all kinds of creativity, especially visual art and haiku; "egocide" as a meaningful alternative to killing oneself; and practicing what he preaches.

He is the author of ten books, including *The Tao of Jung: The Way of Integrity*; *The Healing Spirit of Haiku* with co-author Joel Weishaus; *Transforming Depression: Healing the Soul through Creativity* (now in its third edition); *Medicine as Human Experience* with co-author Dr David Reiser, a classic in the field; the children's book *Henry's Tower;* and *The Tao of Elvis* from Rosenberry Books. Rosen's books have been translated into many languages.

David was born in 1945 in Port Chester, New York, and attended University of California, Berkeley and the University of Missouri School of Medicine, received psychiatric training at the University of California, San Francisco and subsequent training in Jungian analysis. He was the initial holder of the McMillan Professorship in Analytical Psychology at Texas A&M University (the first of its kind in the world), and is now Affiliate Professor in Psychiatry at the Oregon Health & Science University.

Currently living in Eugene, Oregon, with his wife Lanara and their rescued dog Willow, David walks, paints, sees analytic patients, and leads a dream group.

photograph by Erik Verdouw